JOURNEY
TO THE
UNKNOWN
YONIT COHEN

Mike,

A little gift on your B-day as I wish you all that you wish for yourself and MORE!!

Your B-day is the beginning of your own personal year, a new and excited for the journey ahead...

Truly,
Yonit

Praise for the Hebrew version of the book

"Relationships, motherhood, yoga, and a physical and spiritual journey between two worlds. The yoga teacher and Israeli businesswoman, Yonit Cohen, who lives in San Francisco, reveals in her first book, *Journey to the Unknown*, a story that can inspire every woman. In her book, she sincerely unfolds a rich life experience, and manages to navigate between touching descriptions, the ability to look at things from a distance, and formulate for herself quite a few life insights. This is a feminist story of a woman who manages to break free from the shackles of society and expectations, into her own independent path."

~ Israeli Journalist Pini Zohar

"Fascinating reading experience, a sheer pleasure to read this sweeping story. Inspiring book, full of insight into life."

~ Maital Aharoni

"From the moment I started, I could not put it down. I can't remember the last time a book brought me to tears and touched me in places that had been locked for many years."

~ Yehudit C.

"The book is written authentically, with a lot of courage and power."

~ *Zyia Porat*

"Remarkable story! Empowering and inspiring! Daring to tell her personal journey without leaving any detail out. Candid and blunt!"

~*Taly-ann Kirszholc*

Journey to the Unknown

Yonit Cohen

Emery Press, LLC
Fort Lauderdale, FL
www.emerypressbooks.com

First U.S. Edition – November 2020
First published in Israel – July 2020
Translated from Hebrew

ISBN (Print): 978-0-9600505-6-7
ISBN (ebook): 978-0-9600505-7-4

English language translation by Roni Yacobovitz
English language editing by Grammar Goddess Editing
English language cover design by Sweet 15 Designs

In memory of my grandmother,
who always believed that anything was possible,
and who helped me find my way in the world.

Contents

Introduction

Journey to the Unknown is a story about my life, and the choices I made along the way. It's about learning to let go in the hardest way. It's about facing my biggest fear of being alone and navigating through many life conflicts. Conflicts such as identity, belonging, rejection, authenticity, loyalty, and family values. It's about living my values despite all the challenges and saving myself from myself! Along the way, I learned to accept who I am, making friends – and peace – with all the sides of me, some of which I may not be so proud of. And most importantly, it's about overcoming shame.

Chapter 1: The Journey to the Unknown

SO, WHERE SHOULD I BEGIN?

Should I begin the day I was born, in March 1973?

Or perhaps with my childhood days, growing up at my parents' home? Or maybe from the day I enlisted in the army, or the day I left my parents' house after I got married?

Or maybe I should start with the day I began my journey to the unknown, the one that took me to a faraway, foreign country that wonderful, vast country everyone flocks to, dreaming of a perfect happiness that probably only exists in the movies. The United States of America.

Yes, I'll start with that journey to the unknown that had so many surprises in store for me and led me on down numerous complicated paths. The journey that started 20 years ago, and continues challenging and surprising me anew each day.

Life is full of unknown twists and turns, and I will never presume to fathom where they intend to take me, but I still want to believe that everything I tell you here was meant to happen, and every transformation or change was destined to lead me to this point, to the Here and Now.

I always dreamt of writing and telling my story, but the big question always remained – which language to use? Hebrew, my first language, was, of course, the most natural choice, but I sometimes feel that things sound different, or are said more clearly when I use my second language, the language of my children, English. In the end, I decided to tell the story in both languages.

As a native-born Israeli, I grew up in a traditional home with two loving and supporting parents, who taught me the importance of family values and the significance of the land in which I was raised. Friday night Kidush to usher in Shabbat, and Jewish holidays were an inseparable part of tradition in my parents' house, and today, as a mother of teenage twins, I can appreciate the enormous importance of raising children in a supportive, familial, rich tradition.

When I was my sons' age, I was furious at my parents for denying me the right to choose how to spend my Friday nights. I was even jealous of my friends, who were free to do as they pleased. Today, I am grateful for the traditions in which I was raised, and, as a parent myself now, I understand the importance of the education my parents gave me.

Like every other 18-year-old in Israel, I joined the army as soon as I finished high school, and after two years of military service, I started studying for my BA in business management, with a major in accounting. During my four years of college I also married my high school sweetheart, worked as an intern in an accounting firm, bought a house in a developing new suburb in Israel, and adopted my very first dog, Skip.

They were days of prosperity and fulfillment, of lofty dreams that soared to the heavens, and a pure optimism that made us feel invincible, as though everything we wished for was achievable, and the world lay at our feet.

But then something shattered in me.

When I was three months pregnant, I learnt that the fetus in my womb had no pulse, and that I would have to have an abortion. Losing the fetus is pretty common among women in their first pregnancy, but that didn't make the heartbreak any easier to bear.

The irony is that this pregnancy was not planned. We had no intention of becoming parents while we were still so young, so early in our marriage, but when we found out I was pregnant, our hearts were filled with such happiness and joy, and we began preparing for the arrival of the baby.

After the abortion, the one thing I desired, and all I ever thought about, was getting pregnant again. Months went by, and every monthly period brought with it the sorrow and pain of what I had lost.

Even though they undoubtedly meant well and wanted to help, my family only made it worse.

They added fuel to the fire whenever they asked, "So, any news? Are you trying again?"

One day, out of the blue, my husband came up with an idea that quickly transformed into reality – to start anew somewhere else, somewhere far away from Israel, in the United States of America, that great land of opportunity, a faraway continent across an ocean. We would run away from everyone, away from the constant pressure and the obsession of getting pregnant again.

The idea sounded very tempting to me, and without hesitation I took it and ran with it all the way to America; literally.

We settled on the state of California, and within a matter of weeks, I had interviewed for a job located in the heart of Silicon Valley with an accounting firm that was affiliated with the firm I was working for in Israel. With the help of our US firm lawyers, I received a work visa that allowed me to start working there immediately, while my husband awaited his work visa as an immigrant.

It was the year 2000. The last year of the old millennium. The final ovation before the beginning of a new century, a new decade, and a new beginning.

On the 15th of February, in the middle of the night, we landed in San Francisco with our four-year-old dog, Skip. After a very long flight, we expected to be held at the airport in a long Customs line but were surprised to discover that even if we had walked through Security with an elephant or a monkey instead of a dog, no one would have stopped us. Those were very different times, pre-9/11.

Only when we arrived at the hotel did it finally dawn on me what we had done, and in that moment I broke down and cried, filled with regret, fear and anxiety over the unknown in this foreign country.

I will never forget that night, my shaking body and the longing that filled my heart.

The next day, I promised myself that I would do my best to move forward and not look back. That I would do everything in my power to sweeten this journey, and make it wonderful and successful.

And so it was. With my broken English, and a very basic understanding of the accounting rules in the United States, I managed to excel at work and get promoted to manager.

The following year, when the Silicon Valley tech bubble burst and my husband lost his job, I was surprised to learn that my firm was willing to subsidize our living expenses and support us until he found a new job.

In those first few years, we made new friends who soon became like family to us, and my career consumed most of my time and was the center of my life. New experiences, including earthquakes, which are common in California, but not in Israel, became part of our daily routine, and I was quick to learn the social norms – standing in a line instead of in a crowd, respecting another's personal space, and being polite instead of direct – that would help me make my way among the locals.

"Change your place, change your luck" is an old Hebrew saying, and it proved to be true in our case, except for that single thing: my desire to start a family.

Years of fruitless efforts gave rise to tremendous doubts, and I almost gave up hope of ever becoming a mother. Countless treatments by the finest specialists in Stanford only fed the obsession I was preoccupied with day in and day out. I tried to immerse myself in my work, but at the end of every day I still felt that same sense of failure.

After years of failed attempts, we consulted with one of the top specialists in the field, who examined the case thoroughly and informed us that we only had an estimated 2 percent chance of success in trying to get pregnant.

Over the next few days, the dreadful news began to sink in, and with great difficulty we started to come to terms with the fact that adoption might be the only option left to us. Unfortunately, it was well beyond our financial abilities, as was the case with artificial fertilization.

When we learned that our medical insurance did not cover the cost of artificial fertilization, and each attempt could cost a fortune, we almost gave up hope.

But then my darling mother asked me to send her my medical records so that she could get a second opinion from one of the specialists in Israel.

What I did not know at the time was that as an Israeli citizen I was entitled to full funding of all fertility procedures until I was able to get pregnant and give birth to two healthy children. My mother knew this and scheduled a consultation with one of Israel's most renowned specialists.

When she walked into his office with my medical file, the doctor stared at her and said, "I've seen all kinds of things in my line of work, Ma'am, but I have to ask, are you sure you want to try and get pregnant at your age?"

My mother laughed heartily while trying to explain that she was there to talk about her daughter who was shy of 30.

"So, where is she? Why isn't she here?" the doctor sighed.

"She lives in California," my mother sighed back. "Can you help her?"

To her surprise and delight, the doctor did not send her away that day, but instead scheduled a phone conversation with me in order to get more details, and explain the procedure to me and my husband over the phone. We learned that he could mail us all of the necessary medication that would have cost us a fortune here in California, and he would guide us through the process so that we would only have to go to Israel for the fertilization itself.

When the day came, we flew to Israel to meet our doctor at the hospital for the egg retrieval procedure. As luck would have it, I was very fertile and we retrieved 20 eggs, out of which 11 were successfully fertilized.

When we were back at the hospital for the embryo transfer, the doctor wanted to know how many embryos we would like to put back in, hoping one of them planted successfully.

I will never forget that moment, lying on a hospital bed in the operating room, listening to my husband and the doctor's lengthy and detailed negotiation.

When the doctor insisted we transfer three embryos, my husband, on the verge of a stroke, replied, "Sir, if you are willing to fly back with us and raise the triplet, then go right ahead, you have my full consent. Otherwise, I will not have you transfer more than one embryo into my wife's womb."

The doctor thought he was joking.

"Are you crazy? Did you come all this way for nothing? I am not putting one back, no way. What if it doesn't succeed? You'll come all the way from California again?"

After a temperamental argument that seemed to go on forever, I suggested a compromise: two embryos. Transfer the two highest-graded embryos with the best chances of survival. I was surprised when the two "rivals" agreed unanimously.

And today I am a mother of twin boys, those two embryos that developed successfully on the first try. A medical miracle, my marvelous children, two treasures, two worlds, this sublime happiness that was awarded me for all eternity.

But before I get ahead of myself, let us go back to that day when the magic was created inside me.

It was the eve of the Jewish holiday of Sukkot (one of the Jewish High Holidays, in which we all gather in a hut, known as Sukkah), and my family had all gathered at my maternal aunt's house to celebrate.

All of a sudden, my dearest grandmother collapsed and was rushed to the hospital with what we later learned was a stroke. With heartbreaking sorrow, we all crowded the hospital corridors, praying for a miracle to bring her back to us, trying to hold on to a shred of hope.

My mother, the only one in our family who knew about my condition, asked my husband to take me back to California, fearing that worrying about my grandmother might put me at risk of losing the baby. After a great deal of convincing, I agreed to get on the plane, only after securing my mother's promise to keep me posted regarding my grandma's condition.

We spoke on the phone every day, but there was no actual news about grandma, who still laid unconscious at the hospital.

After two weeks, I went to see my gynecologist to check whether the transfer was successful. The ultrasound showed that I was indeed pregnant. I asked whether I was pregnant with one or two babies, and the sound of two very strong and healthy heartbeats affirmed that I was indeed pregnant with twins.

I called my mother right away to give her the wonderful news.

"Mom, I'm pregnant with twins!" I said.

With a heartrending catch in her voice, my mother replied, "Grandma died today."

Chapter 2: Bittersweet

THE FIRST FEW DAYS after we learned I was pregnant with twins the house was full of emotional turmoil. Twins! We were not quite ready for that. Joy blended with worry; we lived so far away from both our families and raising twin babies without the help and support of an extended family seemed like a daunting task.

The thought of multifetal pregnancy reduction did cross our minds, but we gave it up immediately; we were not willing to take a risk.

One day I walked in the house and found my husband sitting on our couch reading a book called *Raising Twins: Parenting Multiples from Pregnancy Through the School Years* by Shelly Vaziri Flais, MD, FAAP.

I realized in that moment that he had assimilated and accepted this new reality. My anxiety settled at bit at the realization. Everything would be okay. Together, we could do this.

I was distressed not to be able to attend my grandmother's funeral. Nor was I able to be there to mark the end of the 30-day morning period. My sorrow over her passing, which was mixed with immense joy, faded as I prepared for the birth of my babies, and every month of my pregnancy was new and exciting for me.

Our blissful anticipation of the arrival of our miracle babies grew. The two heartbeats of the two fetuses, who turned out to be two boys, Baby A and Baby B, as the doctors used to call them, filled our hearts with great happiness and endless love.

Monitoring the pregnancy and preparing for the birth occupied most of our days, and that magical time passed with no particular difficulties, until the day we were informed by our landlord that he intended to put the house up for sale and we must leave.

I was eight months pregnant, which left us little choice but to buy the place.

More bad news followed when my husband lost his job again and was informed that he must leave the country within 30 days.

Doing my best to stay calm, I consulted with my firm's lawyers, who found a way to help us and flew my husband out to Canada to re-enter the United States with a valid working permit as the spouse of a legal alien.

Fortunately, my mother made it to California in time for the birth and was once again my lifeline. She stood by me during 27 hours of intense labor, with her relentless fortitude, compassion, and strength, praying for my sons' health, and weeping for my pain. Tears of joy and grief ran down my mother's face while she prayed for the spirit of my late grandmother.

My mother, who firmly believes in *gilgul*, the reincarnation or "rolling" of the soul through time from one body to a different body, felt certain that the soul of my grandmother – her mother – had given life to my twin sons, who were created on the day she passed away.

What a miraculous transformation! In one day, we went from being a couple with a dog, to a family of four with a dog, and the light that was on day and night filled our home with great warmth and love. Indescribable happiness!

One question I've been asked a lot over the years is, "How did you survive raising twins?"

Well, let me tell you, it's as easy as pie. The secret to our success was "divide and conquer."

We kept a strict schedule during the day, and at night each of us was responsible for feeding one of the boys. Due to selective hearing, we would each respond only to the crying of the baby we were assigned to feed. Fortunately for me, the one I fed ate in four-hour intervals every night, whereas my husband had the tedious task of getting up every two hours to feed the other baby.

The first three months were marked with night shifts and sleeplessness, until finally magic happened and they both slept for the entire night, from 7 p.m. to 7 a.m.

Come to think of it, dividing the workload kept us sane, but the one true secret to our success was a systematic and consistent schedule of regular sleeping habits, including a midday nap that allowed me to study for my California CPA exam and receive my license at the end of my maternity leave, when my boys were six months old.

Going back to work as a new mom was not easy, but my wonderful sister made it possible, giving me the peace of mind of knowing that my sons were in good hands.

My younger sister had just finished her army duty in Israel and agreed to postpone going to college so that she could help us for the first six months of my returning to work, until we were able to find a more permanent arrangement for the boys.

She was born when I was eight. Although I had longed for a baby sister, I was also jealous, worrying that she might be more beautiful than me.

I will never forget the day my father came back from the delivery room, and the first question I asked him was, "Dad, what color are her eyes?"

My father smiled and said, "Brown."

I was so happy and relieved.

I said, "Good. As long as they're not blue or green."

Shortly after my mother came home with the baby, the pent-up jealousy quickly dissipated, and all I wanted was to take care of her like a little mommy. From that day on, my sister became the most precious thing in the world to me.

Now, I was so grateful for her presence in our house, I tried to make her stay with us as pleasant as possible, and to thank her every day. I could not ask for a greater gift than to leave my babies with their aunt, who loved them without condition, and cared for them as her own.

When my babies were a year old, my sister went back to Israel, and we went into a daily routine of dropping them off and picking them up from daycare, feeding, bedtime, shopping, errands, and work, of course, but even with all that, I was so grateful for the joy that came into my life and filled my heart with this huge love.

During that time of my life, I had the habit of looking at everything through rose-colored glasses. I could only see how happy and blooming our little family was. Sadly, I failed to notice the growing distance between my husband and I, until the day I came home to an empty house.

My husband rented an apartment and moved out. The letter he left behind contained some harsh, accusatory statements. This sudden and devastating development took my breath away. I read the letter again and again, anxiety filling my mind as I tried to figure out what had happened.

My boys were then only 14 months old.

In that long letter he related how he always felt like a shadow in our relationship, how becoming a father only strengthened that feeling and brought a new sense of hostility towards me, a hostility that took the form of resentment and jealousy. As the saying goes "Jealousy is as cruel as the grave."

He explained in his letter that he'd had doubts about our relationship for years, but it was our joint parenthood that brought him to the edge and made him throw in the towel.

I was astonished and dismayed at his words. Every time I finished reading that letter, I asked myself, "How did you not see the writing on the wall? Were you living in utter delusion?"

Every day I blamed myself for bringing him to that state of helplessness. Shame and sorrow filled my heart, and I confided in no one except my closest friends. I kept this even from my family; I didn't want to worry them.

I was left alone with two toddlers, trying to hold the reins and praying every day for the return of my husband, my dearest love.

I refused to ask for help from my family who lived so far away, and I tried to hide what was happening at home, hoping and praying that somehow, everything would soon be right again. Compassionate to my husband's emotional state, I tried to support him by giving him the room he seemed to need, while making it clear that I was hoping and waiting for him to return one day.

I finally saw a light at the end of the tunnel when my husband agreed to go to couples' therapy. Our weekly sessions with the therapist brought more hope that we could bridge our differences.

After six months of discussions and sessions, he came back to me, and for a moment, I was once again happy and grateful.

Chapter 3: The Bottomless Bucket

IT HAD BEEN TWO YEARS since my sons were born, and the race for partnership in the accounting firm I worked for was preventing me from enjoying the experience of raising them during the most meaningful years of their lives.

The struggle between career and motherhood came to an end the day I met a woman who was the VP of Marketing for an international high-tech company.

We were sitting at the same dinner table at a friend's wedding, and she was telling all of us around the table what had happened a few days before when she tried to pick her son up from daycare. With tears in her eyes, she shared that when she arrived at the daycare center, the guard asked to see her ID because he didn't recognize her and wouldn't believe that she was the child's mother. When she finished telling the story, tears were streaming down her face, and I felt an ache in my heart in empathy for her pain.

All of a sudden, a lightbulb switched on in my head. I realized this could happen to me if I continued working around the clock instead of spending time with my children. That night I promised myself that I would stop chasing a partnership with the firm and try to find a job that would allow me to spend more time at home.

In the fall of 2005, I handed in my resignation, and with mixed emotions, said goodbye to my coworkers, who had been like family to me.

I started a new job with reasonable hours and a much shorter commute, and for the first time I was able to pick my kids up every day and spend evenings and weekends with them without disturbances. In my spare time, I was even able to get certified as a fitness instructor, which has always been a dream of mine. My certificate allowed me to be a gym instructor, including spinning and toning classes, and soon I was teaching classes on evenings and weekends and enjoying it very much.

As far as I was concerned, everything was perfect again. I was in my mid-thirties, physically fit, and full of gratitude for my wonderful family.

It had been a year since my husband moved back in with us, and I didn't want to be in the dark again, so I asked him to share his feelings with me. He admitted that he wasn't happy. After much persuasion and pleading on my part, he agreed to go back to his weekly sessions with his therapist.

As I wasn't quite sure what to do, I started looking for ways to help him and to lift his spirit. Unfortunately, it was a few more years before I finally understood that the only person who could make my husband happy was himself, and only he had the ability to diminish his suffering. In the meantime, I was channeling all of my energy to fill his life – and ours as a family – with amazing experiences and dreams-come-true.

I made a concentrated effort to create an alternate reality in which the children no longer took priority and we were once again newlyweds who went out and partied all night, and had fascinating new experiences every day. Dreams – such as getting an SUV and going on road trips or getting that flying permit he'd always dreamed of – were expensive, but worth it for me. All I wanted was to see him happy.

We lived like there was no tomorrow, spending and squandering without boundaries, to no avail; my husband's happiness was always temporary, and after a while he would sink back into depression. A depression that made him want to escape reality and distance himself for long periods of time from me and the children.

The bucket remained empty, despite my repeated efforts to keep it full.

The boys turned four, and I was overjoyed to welcome my parents for a visit. They helped us arrange a lavish birthday party with pony-back riding and a picnic in the park with all of our friends and family.

I was so happy that my parents came all the way from Israel to celebrate with us, but what I didn't know at the time was that my husband was just waiting for them to leave so that he could pack his things and leave. Again.

The feelings of shame and failure were almost too much for me to bear. It felt final this time. He signed a one-year lease on an apartment and wanted us to agree on a regular arrangement for him to visit the children, and for them to stay with him on some nights and weekends.

It was in June 2007, the beginning of a bitter and "cold" summer.

The breaking point came in September of that year, when I decided to take the boys to Israel for the holidays.

Yom Kippur, the Jewish Holiday of Atonement – which was greyer than usual in Israel that year – became a time of self-reflection for me, and for the first time in my life, I allowed myself to break down. I stopped trying to be strong and pretend that I was fine; I stopped trying to hide my pain. I gave up trying to embellish everything. I collapsed on my bed in my childhood room at my parents' house. For days I refused to eat or drink, and would not see or talk to anyone, including my children.

One morning I overheard one of my sons say to the other:

"You know, we don't have a mommy or daddy anymore. Now we only have a grandpa and grandma."

My heart was crushed hearing those words. I rose from my bed at once and booked us tickets back to San Francisco. I asked my mother to join us, and she was so worried about me, she agreed without question.

Coming back to San Francisco was much harder than I expected. I lost a lot of weight, and for days I walked around the house like a ghost, sleep deprived and with no appetite. My mother slept with me in my bed, and helped me in the darkest hours of the night, holding me tight when I sobbed in immense anxiety and pain.

One night, I got out of bed in the middle of the night, and, trying my best to not wake her, went to my study and sat at my computer. I booked a ticket for her back to Israel, and it felt like the soundest thing I had done in a while.

My dearest mother only wanted to help her daughter, who was so lost, but she was lost herself, in a foreign country where she didn't speak the language, dependent on me for everything. I realized how much she missed my father and the rest of our family in Israel.

That morning I got up and dressed, put on some makeup and tried my best to put my mother's mind at ease, to show her that I was fine, and that it wasn't necessary anymore for her to stay with me.

I promised my mother that I was much stronger than I seemed, and from that moment on, I intended to get myself together and take good care of myself, a promise that I would – eventually – keep.

Chapter 4: Trying to Move On

SO, LET US PAUSE for a moment in this story and go back to when I met my husband. It was in 1988; yes, when dinosaurs still roamed the earth. We went to the same high school. I was a freshman, he was a sophomore, and he was, in an ironic twist, quite interested in one of my classmates. The feeling wasn't mutual, and since he was looking for an excuse to be around her, he ended up spending most of his recesses with me.

You might think it's pathetic, but in my defense, I was a 15-year-old girl in desperate love with a 16-year-old boy who was so adorable and charismatic, and so nice to me. I dreamt of the moment he would forget about that other girl and fall in love with me.

One day there was a knock at our door. When my mother opened the door, there he was, that dream boy, smiling from ear-to-ear. He asked my mother's permission to take me on a road trip that he and his friends had planned for the day. I went with mixed feelings, knowing full well that all of this was aimed at getting that girl he desired, but I did my best not to reveal my feelings for him. What I didn't know, and couldn't possibly have guessed, was the pleasant surprise that awaited me on the way home.

At dusk we took the last train back to Tel Aviv, all crowding together in the cart that was packed with people. I had closed my eyes and dosed off, when I suddenly felt the touch of a hand stroking mine. I opened my eyes to realize it was *his* hand. My heart started beating hard and a flood of happiness washed through my body.

The following weekend he asked me out, and for my birthday that same week, he bought me a delicate silver necklace with a heart-shaped pendant, which, to me, was a symbol for the beginning of a great love story.

In 1995, when we graduated from college after almost eight years together, we got married.

———————

After my mother left, I went back to my daily routine of working and raising my children.

A few weeks later, a friend suggested that we go to a "meetup" group meeting. I agreed without hesitation, thinking that it was a good idea for me to go out and meet new people.

In that first meeting, I noticed this one guy who I thought was interesting, and he pursued me with single-minded determination, calling and texting me daily until one night he showed up at my spinning class.

I was so charmed by his looks and his persistence that I agreed to go out with him the following Saturday night. We went to see a play in the city. That night turned out to be a very romantic evening with a man who was, as I found out, eight years younger than me.

As much as it may be hard for me to admit, that relationship made me stronger and gave me new hope that I might still be able to move forward and get over the loss of my failed marriage.

I was desirable and wanted once again, and the bitter feelings of rejection that had lingered since my husband left started to dissipate. At 34, I was feeling those same butterflies in my stomach and the same excitement that 16-year-old girl once felt.

I was no longer the poor abandoned woman, but rather a spirited, glowing woman full of renewed energy and optimism.

One morning my husband arrived at our house to visit the boys, and as soon as he walked in, he saw the two wine glasses that my gentleman courter and I had left in the sink the night before. I noticed how in a single moment he became curious and jealous, as he tried to understand what it meant, and to figure out whether I was seeing someone.

Those feelings of jealousy that sparked in him that morning transformed him. The man who had abandoned me a few months before was now romantically chasing me. For the first time in a long time, my husband was pursuing me, and I couldn't have been happier. After all, this was all I wanted – for him to see me once again with the luminous light of desire.

And I was indeed luminous, sought after, holding both sets of reins, enjoying both men, who showered me with love and passion. But deep down, all I really wanted was to win him back; my life companion, my high school sweetheart.

Who would have thought then that in time I would learn that my husband saw himself to be the victim in that situation, betrayed and lied to?

He will forever hold against me that I was able to move on and be with another man.

On New Year's Eve of that year, I went on a romantic trip to New York City with my young admirer, and as all good things must come to an end, I told him that I'd decided to go back to my husband and reunite my family.

I will be forever grateful to him for being there right when I needed him, to help me realize that I am willing and able to step forward.

Chapter 5: The Betrayal

WITH FIVE-YEAR-OLD TWINS, and skyrocketing debt that we had accumulated from having two households for almost a year, my husband's return was somewhat of a financial challenge. But what was even harder for me was the feeling that I had betrayed his trust by moving on so quickly, while he claimed to have always known that the breakup was temporary and that he would soon be back home.

"Didn't you notice I never took my coats from the closet?" he would ask me. "I knew I was going to come home before the winter," he told me again and again.

How could I have known? I asked myself. This time our separation had felt final. I still had such compassion for him, and all I wanted was to earn his forgiveness and regain his trust.

In order to bridge the gap between us, I suggested we again go to couples' therapy, but it was futile. Every session ended on the same note – I, alone, was guilty of this situation because I had been unfaithful. Like a plate of precious china that had been cracked beyond repair, I was now worthless to him.

Yes, amazing as it may seem, I allowed him to place all of the blame upon me. I know how unbelievable and unjust this sounds, but justice was not my first priority in those days. All I wanted was a second chance to start afresh and rebuild our relationship.

Days, weeks and months went by, and I remained that same broken china, a precious thing that was lost to him forever. He claimed that I was the first woman he'd ever slept with (he was the first man I had ever slept with), and that he had never been with another woman. And so that pure thing he once had was now lost, and nothing in the world could bring it back.

Even though this narrative marked me as damaged goods, I tried not to lose hope and to keep our regular sessions with our therapist, while also trying to face this new reality of enormous debt, and how hard we would have to work in order to close the gap.

We came up with different ideas of how to close the debt we accumulated, one of which was opening a side business that we could run while working full time at our jobs. With a kind of brave stupidity, as our lawyers will later describe it, we bought a fancy hair salon in downtown San Francisco from a hairdresser who was ready to retire. With no previous experience in running a hair salon, or any other business for that matter, we bought the place from her, well aware of the risk of losing all of the clientele the moment she retired.

It was a challenging year, in the wake of the 2008 banking crisis (the Great Recession), and many of our clients, who had recently lost their jobs, could no longer afford our services. We made some failed attempts to bring in more business by offering more services, but we only sank deeper into debt. We lost $60,000 of my father's money that he invested in the business, and the financial struggle to keep the place running became impossible.

Our monthly salaries all went to paying the rent and the employees who still worked at the salon, and so basic necessities such as milk and bread for the children became luxuries in our house.

In an effort to cut expenses, I took it upon myself to run the business, and quickly found myself at the mercy of the hairdressers, who came and went as they pleased, and eventually started working for our competitors, taking their clients with them.

In the end, without giving us any notice, they all left, leaving us with one hairdresser and no income to keep the business open. The only thing to do was to find a buyer who would take the place off our hands and free us from the impossible burden of paying that ridiculously high rent every month.

We had to answer to a harsh landlord, and so we were at the mercy of potential buyers and had to sell to anyone who was willing to take the place as is. We eventually gave it away and ended up losing a great deal of money in that transaction.

Still, we felt enormous relief when we transferred ownership to the buyer, and we could only agree with our lawyers who called this failed attempt "expensive education."

Financially, we had hit rock bottom. We were floating in a sea of debt, and emotionally we were left with the bitter taste of defeat, knowing that we failed in the attempt to be self-employed and run our own business.

The most important thing for me at that point was being able to pay my father back. Nothing took priority over this one mission – to pay back every cent of his pension money that he had lost supporting our failed venture. And so, whenever I wasn't at the office, I was teaching a class at the gym. I was working every single moment and cutting any expenses that weren't absolutely necessary.

After a year of hard work, I managed to pay my Dad back in full and felt enormous relief. I wrote him a long letter, describing this financial misadventure, and the daily challenge of facing my husband's hostility. I thanked my father from the bottom of my heart for all the help and support he had given me, and for coming to my aid at this time of crisis.

A few weeks later, I received a reply from my Dad:

> "My darling daughter,
>
> I was so moved to receive your letter. It took me back to a time, so many years ago, when you were a little girl and you would write letters to me. I miss getting letters from you. Your handwriting made me nostalgic, and from the way you express yourself in writing, I could feel the change in you. You're more mature in how you

approach life, and you were always mature for your age.

When I read your letter, I felt the burden you are carrying, navigating your ship through the stormy sea of life. I know it hasn't been easy for you, but you've managed to sail your ship safely to shore by carrying everything on your shoulders.

My darling daughter, I am proud of you, and I know how hard it has been for you. You made it through all these ups and downs like a rock, never giving up, always knowing how to pick yourself up again.

We only ever understand life when we look back on it. There is always another goal, it never ends. In life, as with food, there are three stages: raw, cooked and burned. But life is sweet, and you must keep looking forward.

It hurts me to not have been there for you. But unfortunately, you went so far away. But I am proud of you. You faced that challenge and coped with it. As they say, one should know failure in order to taste victory.

I hope time will heal your wounds, and that every downfall will make you stronger.

Yours, with love,

Dad"

March 12th, 2010

Chapter 6: A New Decade

A NEW DECADE brought new optimism and hope that if we made it through a failed business, we could make it through everything, together, as a family.

The boys started elementary school, and we were as proud as can be. With all the storms and downturns we'd been through, the boys were growing to be very talented and mature for their age. And with that, we drew strength from the commitment we made as parents to try and recover from past failures, and not let the heavy load that we were carrying in our hearts to drag us down.

As a CPA (Certified Public Accountant), the shameful last resort of bankruptcy wasn't an option for me, and we had no choice but to pay back all the debt accumulated over the years, debt that had continued to grow after we closed the business.

But all this hardship and misfortune seemed so minute once I found out that my mother was sick, diagnosed with a rare form of heart infection.

My journey in this foreign country came to an end when my mother got sick, but the dilemma of where to raise my kids had existed since the day they were born. Now, after experiencing the recession, I no longer felt safe raising a family in a country where so many families lost their homes and struggled to survive each day.

When my father told me that my mother was fighting for her life, I knew that if I returned with her grandchildren to live in Israel, it would bring her hope and strength to recover. All I wanted was to go back home, to be closer to everyone, to give my mother a reason to battle this horrible disease that had invaded her weak body without warning.

Although it was clear to me that going back to Israel was the only option, there were many unforeseeable challenges and obstacles to overcome.

First, I had to find a way to pay off all our debt, because I could not leave the country without paying it in full. The remaining outstanding debt, which was now a balance of $120,000, was being paid in small monthly payments, and as I explained to my husband time and again, if we filed for bankruptcy I would lose my license and that would be the end of my career as an accountant. The only option was to use all of our savings, including our 401K pension funds, to pay our debts.

Now all that was left to do was to find jobs in Israel so that we could support ourselves and raise the boys.

I was spending most of my time interviewing for jobs and looking for housing in Israel, and with every step forward I felt my husband retreating from the decision to move back.

When it came time to leave, I was blind-sided by my husband's decision to stay.

"When your journey to Israel fails, I will be here in California waiting for you," he said.

I did not see that coming!!

Raising my children alone in Tel Aviv while he stayed behind hoping for my failure? Was I dreaming?

In the summer of 2011, we made *Aliyah* (Hebrew for "ascent") to Israel, me and my twin boys, who had just turned eight.

With mixed feelings, we said goodbye to my husband and started our lives in Tel Aviv, in a small apartment located in the center of the city, surrounded by the love of our entire family who couldn't wait for us to come home.

But what surprised me most was that my mother not only made a complete recovery, but she worked hard with my father to have the apartment beautifully furnished and cleaned up for our arrival.

It was a great miracle, getting to see my mother recover from her illness, stronger than ever and thrilled with our return.

I guess miracles still happen. I only need to believe.

Chapter 7: *Oleh Hadash* (New Immigrant)

SUMMER 2011, BEN GURION AIRPORT. We made *Aliyah* and became new immigrants.

You see, even though my children and I held dual citizenship in the United States and Israel, when an expatriate returns to live in Israel, it is common to refer to them as a "new immigrant" while they reacclimate to the culture and language of Israel.

I relished my new status.

Sometimes we say, "Expectations lead to disappointment" (expect nothing and you will never be disappointed). But not this time!

We had been longing for this moment for almost a year, dreaming of how wonderful it would be, and we were still pleasantly surprised.

Landing was smoother than I expected, followed by a warm welcome at the airport from our entire family.

We arrived at a high-rise building located in the center of the city to find our apartment on the 27th floor, fully furnished and stocked with every necessity and luxury. It had a view of the Mediterranean Sea and wonderful, fresh air all around.

My sons, who were born and raised in California, were now faced with a different culture and a different language, and to my surprise, their adjustment was smoother than my own.

On the first day of summer camp, I was so anxious about them, I left work early to pick them up, only to find that they had already made plans with a new friend to go to his house.

I was astonished by this kind invitation from their friend's mother, who I had never met (I guess things were done differently here than what I was accustomed to), and asked again whether it was really okay for them to go on such short notice.

"What time should I pick them up?" I asked.

The mother, who in time would become my closest friend in Israel, answered, "Why don't I give you a call when they're done with dinner?"

Dinner? Not only was she inviting them over to play with her son, but she also wanted them to stay for dinner? Both of them?

I was a strange bird in my home country, the place I had left back in my twenties. The boys were not the only ones who had to learn and adjust. Everything I knew, everything I was familiar with as a parent in California revealed itself to be quite different here in Israel.

The openness, directness, maybe even boldness I was once accustomed to was now a new culture I had to adjust to.

I guess there's a logical reason they call us "new immigrants."

I was constantly amazed at how quick the boys were to adapt. And they learned the language in no time. For the first time, they found themselves surrounded by kids who longed for their companionship. New friends from school opened their homes to us, and we did so in return. In no time, our home was filled with playful kids who spent their afternoons with my sons.

And so, my sons blossomed socially, gained some independence, and felt like they belonged. They were free to be themselves, celebrating the same holidays as everybody else, following the same ideals, no longer different, no longer needing to explain why they couldn't go to school on Yom Kippur, or why they didn't celebrate Christmas.

Time flew by, and we hadn't seen my husband in three months. The children and I all missed him terribly. After a great deal of persuasion over the phone, he agreed to come and spend the Jewish High Holidays with us.

His plane landed right after Yom Kippur, and the three of us, excited as could be, went to meet him at the airport.

Little did I know that his visit was a campaign. Put simply: as soon as he landed, he started pleading with us to pack our bags and return to California with him.

By the end of his visit, we agreed to disagree, and though we were saddened to do so, once again parted ways.

In December of that year, I was given the opportunity to go to a work conference in Washington D.C., and the first thing that came into my mind was to offer my husband to meet me there so that we could spend the week together. I yearned to see him and spend time with him.

That trip turned into the perfect romantic week in this fascinating city, the center of the US federal government.

It was our 16th wedding anniversary, and we celebrated it like we were on our second honeymoon, with enormous love. Inseparable, we held each other all night, talking, laughing, dreaming of the moment we'd be together again. Being together, so close to each other, filled me with faith that we still had that great love and a deep connection.

We hugged at the airport, tears in our eyes, not wanting to let go of each other, but we had to go our separate ways again. I boarded a plane to Tel Aviv, and my husband flew back to San Francisco.

I was home once again – still an immigrant, but with the hope that this was where we belonged, and with a dream that one day my husband would come to his senses and join us in Israel.

Chapter 8: Whoever Blinks First

LIFE IN ISRAEL was taking on a routine and I was even able to continue teaching spinning and toning classes at a local gym.

As a single mother in Israel, my biggest concern was providing for my family while living in such an expensive city as Tel Aviv.

Everyone around us was quick to help out with babysitting, picking up the boys from school, cooking and errands, which was crucial for me in raising the boys while being absorbed in developing a new career.

I tried hard not to worry too much and just enjoy the moments, but every night, at exactly 10 p.m., the phone rang and my husband's voice on the other end of the line heightened all the doubts and concerns that I already faced.

Doubts about our relationship, doubts about his role in our lives as the father of my children, doubts about the possibility of him finding work in Israel and my future in Israel as a single provider, doubts about raising my children without a father.

I wondered, who will be the first to cave?

For my 39th birthday, my lovely family organized a wonderful surprise party. The best part of the party was when I opened the giant present in the middle of my parents' living room, and my sweet boys jumped out of the package and gave me the most loving hugs. I melted.

There was enormous love inside of me, and it created a magical circle of new friends – our neighbors, parents at the school, work colleagues, fellow gym instructors and so many more.

But every night, that feeling of belonging shattered to pieces once the phone rang. The 10 p.m. calls coincided with my husband's lunch break, and the time difference between Tel Aviv and San Francisco seemed greater than ever.

Those conversations led nowhere, and often ended in the small hours of the night. Night after night we mined endless furrows around the same topic, each trying to convince the other to come, to the point of exhaustion.

Each successive conversation was more draining than the last, and the emotional canyon between us widened.

A year passed, and the distance had its effect.

The status of being a married woman while my husband was living on a different continent felt weird to me, and even though I wouldn't admit it, I was lying to everyone around me.

I knew my husband would never come to Israel to live with us.

The school year ended, and my husband asked if the boys could come spend the summer with him. I felt obligated to say yes, and with a heavy heart, agreed for them to go to California for two months, which at the time seemed like forever to me.

On June 26th, 2012, at 1 a.m., I put my two boys on a direct flight to LA with a supervising flight attendant, hoping and praying that their flight would be quick and easy.

That very night, after I parted with them, I knew that this was not what I wanted for my children. I didn't want to keep making them live like this, torn between two worlds.

For the first time since the twins were born, I was on my own, without any commitments or concerns. Just me and myself.

The first week was full of fun. I hung out with friends, and enjoyed my time off and the sudden gift of freedom, but after a couple of weeks, I missed the boys so much, I found myself calling every day to check in on them and talk to them.

I hated the feeling of being distant from my family, and even more so the circumstances that led us to this situation. I was counting the days, waiting for their return, always fearful they would suddenly change their minds and decide to stay in California, the place of their birth, where they were raised, in their familiar bedroom, full of childhood memories.

During that time of great uncertainty and doubt about my future, my employer at the gym sent me to a yoga workshop, which at the time seemed less like a privilege and more like a burden. In time, I became forever grateful for the first taste of yoga I was given that day.

It was one of those typically hot Saturdays at the end of August, when most people are at the beach and not working out at the gym, but in the end, I was glad to have attended.

To my amazement, the connection I felt to the instructor and her teachings transformed my perception about yoga, and about myself.

At the end of the day, I approached the instructor and asked if she could give me private yoga lessons. I was thrilled when she agreed.

And so, every Tuesday night she would come to my apartment for a blessed hour of inward focus and hard work, unfolding the sacred elements of this beautiful new world, a world of self-study and connection to my inner voice.

Finally, the day arrived that my sons returned home. I waited for them at the airport arrival gate, scanning each passenger, and suddenly I saw two tall boys with California tans running towards me. For a split second I didn't recognize them (my heart pinched), and then, with a huge smile and open arms, I took them in, holding them tight for a long moment.

I was so excited to see them, I didn't even notice the flight attendant who stood right next to us. Following his protocols, he asked to see my ID to confirm that I was indeed their mother.

What I didn't expect was their honest opinion as soon as we got into the car to drive home.

"Mom, your car is so old," one of them said. "Dad's car is better."

And the other added, "Mom, I like living with Dad better; I hate living here."

Now on top of the difficulty of getting readjusted, they also had the hardship of missing their father, and it wasn't long before I realized that they were torn between two worlds and two parents living so far away from each other.

They started 4th grade, and I supported them as much as I possibly could in getting back on track.

I focused on trying to maintain a daily routine, but doubts lingered, and the tension between me and my husband sprouted like weeds.

In an effort to find the right answer to the dilemma of our geographical distance, I tried to disconnect from all of the background noises and direct my focus inwards. With the help of yoga and swimming, I was able to ignore the confusion and uncertainty of our circumstances and concentrate on my inner voice and my intuition.

On the Eve of Yom Kippur 2012, I walked with my sons through the empty streets of Tel Aviv. The custom in Israel is that on Yom Kippur everything shuts down and no one drives their cars. The roads, including the main highways, are closed. People can stroll in the middle of the road, and kids can ride their bicycles.

We meandered through the streets in that wonderful atmosphere, absorbing the amazing tradition of that special day and the way it is observed in Israel, walking and talking about the many differences between life in Israel and life in the US.

While I listened to my children, trying to attune my ears and heart to their feelings and not just their words, I realized I had to make a difficult decision.

I was in emotional turmoil throughout that day, and when the fast ended, I knew what I had to do. The main difficulty was how to tell everyone, and how to carry out what I knew was best for my children.

My father always said to me: "You always know what to do, and nothing stands in your way when you really want something."

Exactly two weeks from the day I made the decision, I sold the entire contents of our apartment, found a new tenant, and with six suitcases packed with our belongings, we flew back to our home in California.

Yes, I was the one who blinked first.

Chapter 9: Returning to California

ON OCTOBER 23RD, 2012, after a very long flight, we landed at the San Francisco airport.

With no real direction, and absolute faith, I fell into my husband's arms with a sigh of happiness and relief.

I wasn't alone anymore!

We drove back to the house in Redwood Shores, a suburban neighborhood 20 minutes outside of San Francisco, that same house I'd left 18 months before, thinking I would never see it again.

The outside of the house looked exactly like I remembered it, but when I walked through the front door, I felt faint. The white walls, now painted in red and yellow, were molding, and piles of dirt and garbage were everywhere.

I almost did not recognize the place. My eyes welled with tears.

I quickly came to my senses and suggested to my husband that he and the boys go to the pool while I unpacked our bags and cleaned up the house. This kept me busy for most of the day, and I managed to avoid falling over the cliff of regret.

By the end of the day, every surface was gleaming, and the familiar scent of home filled the air.

We were all happily exhausted, so we went to bed early, but in the middle of the night I woke up, jetlagged, and somewhat panicked, trying to figure out where I was and whether I was dreaming or really lying in bed next to my husband.

I felt an anxiety attack looming, and so I woke my husband, hoping he would comfort me and tell me how happy he was to have us home.

To my great surprise, he was distant and sounded very different from the man who had called me every night to persuade me to come home.

Confused and horrified, I asked if he would take a walk with me so that I could get some fresh air and try to relieve my anxiety. He agreed and got out of bed to get dressed.

We walked those empty streets. I was still having a hard time believing they were not the streets of Tel Aviv, but a peaceful suburban neighborhood just minutes from San Francisco.

I was looking for a bit of empathy for my situation, some appreciation for the giant leap I took by returning here without any direction, without knowing if and when I would find a job here again.

I was looking for understanding, warmth, and love, but all I got was a cold shoulder, and an inability – or an aversion – to acknowledge what I had to sacrifice in order to reunite us as a family.

I came home to that cold bed, praying for morning, hoping that in the light of day things would look different.

Luckily, I got sidetracked by having to re-enroll the kids in school and help them get back on track.

Less than a week after we landed, I also received some good news: the San Francisco office of the global firm that I had worked for in Israel offered me an exciting, challenging role.

Gradually, my days filled with meetings and errands that helped to reduce the level of anxiety that attacked me when I first returned to the U.S.

Once again, I felt sought after, at least on the career front.

The position I was offered, heading our West Coast region inspection support, meant that I would be overseeing 14 offices and more than 200 partners. It was my dream job, more responsibility and authority than I had taken on to this point in my career, and it put my competency to the test, demanding that I broaden my mastery of the profession.

I love being challenged professionally and felt that it was time for me to focus on my career, hoping that I would be able to make things better at home as well.

Busier than ever, I struggled to maintain my optimism, but the more I blossomed, the more my husband drifted away. I had no idea why the same person who couldn't wait for our return, pining for us day and night, was now acting like a caged lion with no desire to spend his time with his family.

Two months after our arrival, the holidays came, and we were all off for the winter break. Despite the cold weather, it was great to be together again, all of us at home for a while.

This situation made my husband uncomfortable to the point that he sought an opportunity to get away. And so, ignoring the stormy weather, he went biking north of San Francisco, leaving us for the entire holiday season.

Though surprised by his decision, I tried to be supportive. Maybe he needed some time alone; after all, he had been living alone for more than a year. It must have been difficult for him to acclimate to having us underfoot all the time. He was so keen to leave, I felt like we were a burden to him. Maybe it would be best if he went on this trip.

I wanted to believe that he would return with recharged batteries and tons of love to share with us, but that never happened.

Chapter 10: The Other Woman

IT WAS MY 40TH BIRTHDAY, and I felt like my husband was forcing himself to cooperate with my friends, who wanted to throw me a party. The party was on my birthday, March 12th, but the atmosphere was tense, and it was hard for me to fake having fun at my own party.

During dinner, one of my friends asked my husband to raise a toast and say a few words in my honor.

Forced to stand up, my husband raised his glass and said, "May you always stay beautiful."

I didn't quite know how to react at that moment and so, a little embarrassed, I murmured, "Thank you."

My darling boys, who were both there, hugged me, and my aching heart was filled with joy again.

The gift that was waiting for me in the car in a plastic shopping bag with no wrapping paper indicated how incapable my husband was of giving me anything. Even though he was physically with us, his mind was somewhere else.

Summer came, and with it, my husband's 41st birthday. The boys and I planned a camping trip and were ready to celebrate his special day out in nature with a cake and balloons, and many other surprises.

It wasn't clear whether he was happy about the idea of camping and hiking or whether he would rather stay home, but he did cooperate with us. The day before his birthday, we loaded everything into our SUV and hit the road. At night, after my husband fell asleep, the kids and I decorated our camp with balloons and other birthday decorations and waited excitedly for morning.

We woke up early, and with a cake and candles went into his tent to sing "Happy Birthday," and surprise him with a gift.

He opened his eyes, and listened as we sang, accepted his gift, and, with a half-smile, said, "Thank you." But he did not make any attempt to get out of bed and enjoy the celebratory atmosphere we created for him.

My younger son (born 10 minutes after his brother) asked, "Dad, why don't you love mom as much as she loves you?"

My heart was crushed, and I tried my best to hide the embarrassment and sorrow I felt in that moment.

It was a beautiful sunny day, and we tried to enjoy the wild nature all around us. Throughout the day my husband's phone rang, but he wouldn't answer.

When I asked him about it, he just sighed and said, "It's probably from work; I don't want to talk to them on a Saturday."

That night, like so many nights that followed, ended with a heavy silence and distance between us, which gave rise to doubts and questions like, "Why doesn't my husband touch me anymore?; Why is he so distant?; Why can't I find a way into his heart?; What's wrong with me?; Am I so unattractive in bed?"

Endless questions haunted and tortured me.

Summer ended, and the boys started middle school. They had to take public transportation to get to school and back every day, and I was so proud of their independence. I felt hopeful, once again, that we did the right thing coming back here, and that, in the end, everything would work out.

One Saturday morning, I was getting ready to go to a yoga class, and my son asked if he could go with me to the city. His father and his brother were still asleep, and he was bored. I knew that I would probably have to give up yoga that morning, but I was grateful for the opportunity to spend the morning with my son, and so together we headed to the city.

It was a sunny morning and driving into the city was a very pleasant experience. We went to Dolores Park, which we loved, and had breakfast in a cafe facing the park, with the autumn sun lightly touching our faces and a gentle wind blowing.

My phone rang and I answered, thinking that my husband may have woken up and was wondering where we were, but to my surprise it was my other son. He had woken up to find that he was all alone in the house.

"Mom! Where are you?" he asked. "Why did you leave me all alone?"

"We didn't leave you alone," I replied. "Dad is home with you."

"I can't find Dad. He isn't here," my son claimed.

"Are you sure?" I asked. "Did you check the garage?"

"I checked everywhere, Mom! Dad isn't here."

I asked that he go outside to see if his father maybe went to the neighbor's.

Soon he came back and said, "Mom, I can hear him, but I can't see him."

Confused, I asked if his father was maybe outside talking to the neighbors.

He answered, "Mom, I found him! He's in his car, talking on the phone."

When we came home, I asked my husband who he was talking to on the phone.

He said, "My dad."

I was surprised by his answer, but kept quiet, not wanting to ask any more questions that might give away my doubts and went into the kitchen to prepare lunch.

While I was cooking, my husband took the boys to the Jacuzzi and left his cellphone on the kitchen counter. Right after they left, his phone rang, and I looked and saw his father's name on the screen.

I went outside to tell him that his father was looking for him, but he just said, "That's all right, I'll call him back."

At that moment I realized something wasn't right. It was already after midnight in Israel, and if his father was calling at this late hour, it had to be urgent. After a moment, countless text messages started popping on the screen, all of them from his father.

I was curious to know what was so urgent, and so I opened his cell phone, and a long chain of messages was revealed to me.

I couldn't breathe. The more I read, the more I felt sick to my stomach. It appeared to be a lengthy dialogue between my husband and a woman whose name I had yet to discover.

The long text messages expressed their love for each other and their desire to be together again.

It took every ounce of mental strength for me not to lose my mind at that point, and I rushed out of the house.

I felt suffocated and tears were running down my face.

I suddenly grasped that I had been living a dreadful lie all this time, blind to the huge sign that had been hanging on the wall since we came back from Israel.

The sign that said, "My husband has another woman!!!"

Chapter 11: Finding It Hard to Believe

FINDING IT HARD TO BELIEVE all those text messages I had just seen, I confronted my husband to try and find out what he had been hiding from me for months.

I asked if we could talk outside so the boys won't hear us.

He denied that he was having an affair with another woman, explaining that she was a 24-year-old art student he met when the boys and I were living in Israel. Since then, she hadn't left him alone, insisting that they stay in touch.

I asked him to tell me everything, to hold nothing back, but all I got was denial of everything he had written her, and any intentions towards her.

I took a deep breath and asked him to pack his bags and leave the house at once.

I felt cheated, stupid and naive. I started having nightly anxiety attacks again, and I had no appetite. My soul felt dark and empty.

Every part of me wanted to believe my husband, who kept calling and asking for my forgiveness.

I wanted to wake up from this perpetual nightmare. Instead, the torment became even more real.

One night the house phone rang, and on the other end of the line I heard the voice of a young woman.

"Hello. Is Ethan home?"

My heart started pounding and I replied, "May I ask who's calling?"

It got quiet on the other end of the line.

Since I was afraid she might hang up, I asked quickly, "Is this Karen?"

She was silent for a moment, and then said, "Yes."

That night I had a long conversation with that young student who claimed to have had a relationship with my husband for the last two years. In her defense, she did not know he was married. He told her he was divorced and had two kids, and explained that since we came back from Israel, we were just living under the same roof and raising the kids together.

I must say that she sounded very mature for 24, and I was grateful she was willing to tell me everything, including the last time they met and what he told her about me.

I thanked her for her openness and integrity.

Right before she hung up, she said, "I never intended to break a family apart."

I put down the house phone, picked up my cell phone and texted my husband, who had taken the boys to see a movie.

"When you get home, please drop the boys off, and never step into this house again. I never want to see you again!"

When the boys came home, they must have heard me sobbing in my bedroom.

They opened my door and left a drawing they had made for me with a little note that read, "Mom, you have us, we will make you happy."

That night, I bought three plane tickets to Tel Aviv so that I could take the boys on a holiday to visit the family we had missed so much. A little over a year before, I left my extended family and my beautiful apartment in Tel Aviv to reunite with my husband. And here I was, coming back to visit with the children, broken to pieces, not knowing where to go from here.

Trying my best to be in the here and now, and to have fun with the boys, I decided to fly out to Eilat, a resort town on the Red Sea near Jordan, and take them on an introductory scuba dive in the Red Sea.

There is nothing more relaxing than gazing at the sparkling Red Sea, admiring the majestic mountains or practicing yoga at sunrise. That was what gave me the strength to really be present and not dwell in self-pity and endless thoughts about our future.

One morning, when I opened my eyes after a long meditation facing the ocean, I saw two flags waving in the wind – one was the American flag and the other was the Israeli flag. All along, I was looking right at the American Embassy; how symbolic.

Deep down, I knew that was my biggest dilemma – where to settle down. Especially that I was now by myself, a single mother of 10-year-old twins.

Our visit to Israel ended with the New Year, when the boys had to go back to school, and I had to go back to work. We said goodbye to everyone, and after a long flight, we landed in San Francisco, returning to an empty, frozen house.

Our next-door neighbor, who had heard us come in, came to greet us, and I noticed there were tears in her eyes.

She hugged me tight and whispered in my ear, "I'm so sorry... all along I thought that you got divorced when you moved to live in Israel. But you must understand, one day, all of a sudden, there was a different woman in the house."

"What do you mean?" I asked.

"Your husband was living here with another woman. She moved in with her dog, and the dog kept barking. We were so happy to see you back."

I felt dizzy when I realized what she was saying. All that time my husband was living here with his student girlfriend. How would I ever be able to sleep in that bed again, where they had spent every night together while we were away in Israel?

That night I couldn't sleep. I sat down and wrote an email to my therapist, who was my lifeline in those days:

> "Lies. So many lies. I want to scream! He is just toying with my emotions and using my love for him. I just can't believe it. I can't bear to look at his face anymore. He's been having this affair for the last two years, but he's afraid to face the truth, afraid to act, and so he keeps me in limbo, because it is just so convenient for him to have a nice home, and a wife who provides for him, cooks, cleans and takes care of everybody.
>
> He keeps going in circles, keeps accusing me that I haven't changed, anything he can say to justify his behavior, and all this time I have been living in darkness. I keep hoping, keep trying, when anyone else would have given up a long time ago.
>
> Who is this man? Why do I even love him? He's a liar, a coward, a cheater, selfish, and weak! And to think I asked him if he wanted to go out and celebrate our anniversary on December 12th... How dumb can I be?

God only knows why he kept calling me every night while we were living in Israel to try and persuade me to come back.

Now I know that I did everything in my power to keep our family together, and that I am the hero in this story.

I wish it didn't hurt like I'm hurting right now! I really hope that eventually I will heal and will go out into the world stronger than ever. I want to fly and rise up; I want to stop being afraid. I won't let the dark thoughts consume me. I want to move forward and leave fear behind."

January 10th, 2014

_____

The next day I did two very meaningful things. One was ordering a new mattress for my king size bed, and the other was filing for divorce.

My husband didn't take it very well and kept trying to find a way to change my mind. He wrote long letters, describing the remorse he felt; letters that tore at my heart, and made it very difficult for me to make the decision to let him go once and for all.

This was one of my final letters to him:

"Thoughts in sleepless nights.

To you.

Right before I close my eyes, I am writing to you.

Looking back, I see now how you gave me no chance to ever get close to you. What did you call it? No strings attached. And yet, I kept fighting; I never gave up. Respecting your time and your privacy, I waited.

I remember now all those failed attempts to persuade you to go out, just the two of us, to reconnect, to make you see me, see my pain. It was all in vain. You could never see me. You could never be empathetic; you could never stop lying and cheating.

This ability you have to fake love, romance and commitment for so long, this time as well as all the other times you ran away, I see it as complete detachment – uninhibited, immoral, narcissistic – completely disrespectful of any human being, let alone a woman who was only looking to be loved in return.

You always saw me as the enemy, the competition, and you were never really able to enjoy my friendship and my loyalty to you. I always thought I had something special, but reality just hit me in the face, and the man I thought I knew, the man I was so proud of, crushed my innocence and proved how naive I really was.

And why? Why? I ask. Because I have power? Because I know what I want? Because I always get what I want? Because I'm strong? Because I'm driven? Because I love so much that all I ever want is to please and to give? And it hurts so bad; you have no idea.

I built so many false hopes, I weaved so many dreams around someone who no longer dreams about being with me, someone who will hold a grudge against me for the rest of my life.

You write so beautifully, your words are so captivating, the very words I long to hear, but your actions are so severe, so drastic, that they diminish words. Your despicable actions overpower everything you have said.

Goodnight."

January 27th, 2014

Chapter 12: Surgery

I WAS ALWAYS TOLD that only God can make plans, but I never really believed it to be true.

Until the day the phone in my office rang when I was in the middle of an important meeting. My secretary picked up the phone, and after a few seconds popped her head into my office.

"It's the hospital. Your husband is in the ER and they want you to come right away. They're saying it's urgent."

Without a second thought, I grabbed my things and ran to my car.

As soon as I got to the ER, a doctor approached me and asked me to sign a consent form so that they could prep my husband for an emergency operation to remove his gallbladder.

Trying to make sense of what he had just said to me, I asked to know more about my husband's condition, and the surgeon, who overheard us talking, came over and explained how severe his situation was.

"The gallbladder is usually the size of our big toe, but your husband's gallbladder has grown into the size of an orange and is now starting to leak into his liver. If I don't operate on him immediately, he will die".

I signed the consent form and asked to see my husband. The nurses took me to his bed, and as soon as I saw him lying there contorted with pain, I got dizzy and collapsed.

For the first time in my life I fainted.

When I opened my eyes, I saw two nurses standing above me. Looking concerned, they were calling my name, trying to wake me up. One of them kneeled over and asked me to take a sip from the apple juice box she was holding.

"In a split second you got pale as a ghost and then you lost consciousness," one of them explained. "You need sugar! Please drink this juice, I promise you will feel better".

A few minutes later, the surgeon came to take my husband to the OR. In his white coat and with a kind smile he shook my hand, promised that my husband was in good hands and I had nothing to worry about.

Hours in the waiting room felt like eternity.

After seven hours, the surgeon came out to tell me that there had been some complications, but my husband was out of danger. He explained that they succeeded in clearing his body from all toxic residue after they removed his gallbladder, and that he was now in the recovery room.

"A nurse will take you to see him when he wakes up."

I thanked the surgeon, and immediately called my husband's parents in Israel.

"He is out of danger," I said. "I promise that as soon as he wakes up and is able to speak, I'll call you again so you can hear his voice."

That week my life turned around completely. I spent most of my time in the hospital. Our dear neighbor moved in so that she could take care of the boys, and to our great joy, my husband was released from the hospital a week after his operation.

Now nothing was more important than him getting better. It felt like somebody up there was testing and challenging me. Just like in a game of chess, the opponent's moves are out of my control and I am tested time and again – what will she do next?

I was facing a new reality.

After much persuasion, my husband agreed to move back in with us. He needed constant care and help during his recovery. He couldn't drive in his condition, and every day I had to clean and dress his wounds.

This new course of things gave rise to a lot of compassion and a new hope, and I decided to put the divorce process on hold for now and see where this new situation would lead us.

Deep down, I truly believed that this was a sign from the universe that I should forgive him and take him back. After all, we got his life back, and we were once again a happy family.

With everything in me I wanted to believe that this time it would be different.

Chapter 13: Women Who Love Too Much

IT WAS A FEW MONTHS before everything came back to normal.

We were so grateful that my husband was back on his feet, and that everyone was healthy, and everything seemed wonderful again. Except I didn't know what was really happening under the surface. I only saw what was in front of my eyes.

Everyone around me thought I must have lost my mind, bringing him back into my life, but I had a stranglehold on the belief that this time would be different.

My therapist tried to imply several times that "if it walks like a duck and quacks like a duck, it's likely to be a duck..." but I wanted to believe that he could change.

One day, when I was able once again to find some time for myself, I treated myself to a facial at my favorite spa in Palo Alto. I enjoyed the pampering, but even more so, the heart-to-heart conversation with the esthetician beautician, who in time would become like a mother to me and a grandmother to my children.

When we parted, she made me promise to buy the book *Women Who Love Too Much* by Robin Norwood, and read it front to back.

At first, I didn't understand how a book on women who suffer physical and emotional abuse from their male partners could be relevant to me, but I did as I promised. As soon as I left the spa I went to the nearest bookstore and purchased a copy.

Every night before I went to bed, I read a chapter of the book, and day by day I started to notice the similarities between the patterns of behavior detailed in the book and my own situation. I realized how blind I was to my own reality.

Based on the advice of my therapist, I suggested to my husband that we try something we had never tried before: a sex therapist.

I was amazed that my husband agreed to these weekly sessions that cost us $300 for 50 minutes, but felt that this was our last resort. Something we should try before calling it quits, once and for all. We even cut other expenses so that we could continue to afford the sessions. Soon, though, these weekly sessions became a burden for my husband.

In our first session, our therapist explained that his role was no different than a window washer.

"If I do my job right," he explained, "you'll be able to see better when you look out the window.

"All I ask is that you tell me if I did a good job cleaning your windows and you can see things clearer."

We were silent.

And then he added, "I have many patients, and I see no point in wasting my time and your money. If I feel like I can't help you, I will tell you."

The sex therapist continued to remind us, "It is really important that I know both of you want to 'open the same restaurant', otherwise we're really wasting our time."

And then, one night, after about 10 sessions, he said to my husband: "Listen, I don't know what your problem is! I would take your wife home with me right now. Your wife loves and worships you, and yet you keep being miserable and unhappy".

His words are ingrained in my mind; in that moment, I accepted how slim the chances were of saving our marriage.

Chapter 14: Mexico

SOMETIMES THERE IS no reasonable explanation why we do certain things. If there's one thing I'm grateful for during this time of upheaval, it was having the courage to go on a trip to Mexico for a yoga retreat in December 2014.

I spent an entire week in a Mexican jungle with a group of women I had never met before. It was the first time I dared to travel with complete strangers, people who were not my friends or family.

Our destination was Sayulita, a small town 45 minutes north of Puerto Vallarta, and the retreat was held in a place called Haramara, right in the heart of an enormous jungle on a remote beach, with no electricity or internet reception. A dream come true!

I must confess that up until that point, except for the times we went camping, I always stayed in luxurious five-star hotels, and I certainly never imagined myself in wild nature with no electricity, waiting for the sun to come up and light my way, and for the moon to pierce the darkness of my night.

Of course, none of us had any idea why we had to bring a flashlight and batteries, until we got to the campsite and each of us was handed a key to her "Casita."

I bet you're asking, "What's a Casita?"

A casita is a cabin made of wood and straw, with curtained windows that frame the expansive views, and an outdoor shower and toilet. Private and secluded from the other guests, but not from the wildlife.

The host who came to meet us in the reception area escorted us, each to her assigned casita, as the rest of us stood on the trail waving her goodbye. We kept spiraling down towards a clearing in the jungle, until it was down to me and the guide, and I was wondering if I would ever get to my casita. He signaled me to follow him, and we climbed up the trails, crossing two rickety wooden bridges to a remote area, isolated from the rest of the group. He pointed at a huge, beautiful casita that was situated up a staircase and overlooking the ocean.

"Here we are! This is your casita."

Before I had a chance to say anything, he added, "Dinner is served at seven." And then he disappeared.

Shocked, I quickly unpacked, found my flashlight, and before it got dark, began my journey back to the dining area that was located near the entrance of the camp.

I was starving and sweaty when I finally got up there, and I was glad to find my group all sitting together, waiting for me to join them for dinner. When I sat down, I told them about my casita being so remote and my fear that if anything happened to me, no one would be able to hear me or come to my aid. One of the girls suggested I ask the camp manager if I could maybe get a closer casita.

I got up and looked around for the camp manager, who was standing in the entrance to the dining room. I told him that I was terrified to sleep alone in that remote casita, but he just smiled.

"Ma'am, I'm so sorry, we're fully booked at the moment. Your casita is called 'the Diamond', and I know that you're afraid to stay there, but I'm sure there's a reason why you were given that specific casita, because everything happens for a reason."

I stood there, shocked and disappointed.

He kept his smile and went on to say, "I truly hope that by the end of the week you will realize that, too".

I went back to my group and told them that they were fully booked, and I must stay in that casita for the entire week. One of the women suggested I stay with her for the night.

"I'm also really terrified to sleep alone, I heard they have Tejon here…"

"What are Tejon?" I asked. "What kind of animal is that?"

"They're like little bears with the head of a raccoon," one of the other women answered. "They only come to look for food and shiny objects."

That night I was glad I chose to stay with my new friend in her casita, rather than walk all the way back to my remote lodging in pitch black. In the morning, I thanked her for her kind hospitality and started my long walk to my own casita where I had left my things.

Things always look different in daylight, and indeed, when I got to my casita, the sight was no less spectacular than an actual diamond!

It was a piece of paradise, secluded and stunning, with a gorgeous view of the ocean and tropical trees filled with exotic birds chirping and tweeting at the sunrise. In comparison to the other casitas in the camp, this was an actual palace.

I gazed at this breathtaking view from my bed, and promised myself that I would face my fear and sleep there that night.

The first day of the retreat was packed with yoga practices and eye-opening lectures, and after dinner I said goodnight to my group and walked back to my casita with my trusty flashlight lighting the path. To dissipate my fear, I started singing at the top of my lungs, hoping the wild animals would understand that I was just walking to my lodgings and had no intention of hurting them.

"I come in peace!"

I have to admit that I hardly slept at all that first night alone in the jungle. Listening to every hum and murmur that came out of the darkness around me, I prayed that the jungle animals would stay away from my bed. It was pitch black, and the only thing that helped settle my breath and put my turbulent mind at ease was the sound of the waves...

I was wakened out of a sound sleep by loud shrieking sounds that seemed to come from high up in the trees. Realizing that I had eventually fallen asleep, and that the sun was already up, I got up and went to the window to see what all the noise was about.

To my great surprise, I saw a flock of eagles circling the trees around my casita, shrieking and screaming, loudly conversing with each other in the sunrise. My jaw dropped at this magical sight, and for a moment I felt complete peace, as wild nature enveloped me in its majestic beauty and perfection.

Let me explain something about myself – I'm a terrible coward. My greatest fear is snakes. Close on their heels are cockroaches, which I call "garbage insects" because whenever I go to take the garbage out, they're right there, disgustingly lurking in the garbage room.

I will never forget the one Saturday night when my parents left my brother and me at home alone. I was eight years old and my brother was 12. It was a hot summer evening and the living room window was wide open to let in some air. My brother and I were watching TV, when suddenly a huge cockroach flew in through the window. We both jumped off the couch screaming, trying to escape the bug that was flying across the room. My brother opened the front door of our apartment and we both went out into the hall, locking the door behind us, so that the bug won't follow.

When my parents came home that night, they found me and my brother sitting on the stairs outside waiting for them. When they heard the story of how we got locked out, they laughed heartily, and my dad whispered: "I think you scared the cockroach so much, it probably flew out the window by now. Let's all go inside and go to bed."

––––––––––––

The week I spent in Haramara had many once-in-a-lifetime experiences in store for me. We went whale-watching and scuba diving, finding hidden caves at the bottom of the ocean. I will be forever grateful for these unforgettable experiences and the opportunity I was given to be part of this amazing retreat.

The Hebrew word for "opportunity" is hiz'dam'nut (HIZ-DAM-NOOT). The same Hebrew letters that spell this word, also spell three other words in Hebrew that mean "time," "gift," and "thank you."

So, I am thankful for this time in Haramara that was given to me as a wonderfully blessed gift.

But most importantly, I discovered why I got the most remote and secluded casita in the camp. It was to prove to myself that I can face another of my greatest fears – being alone – and to believe that nothing terrible would happen if I only trusted myself and stayed peaceful.

I spent the last few hours of my trip before leaving for the airport sitting outside my beautiful casita, taking in the fresh air in this small piece of heaven that was lent to me for that one week. I felt like the luckiest person on earth, going back home to my family with recharged batteries and newfound strength I didn't know I had in me.

Chapter 15: Neo the Cat

THERE ARE CAT PEOPLE and there are dog people. I am definitely a dog person. It was my childhood dream to have a dog, and the first thing I did after I got married was adopt Skip. When we lived in Israel, before the twins were born, Skip was our pride and joy and our "only child." He was a very special dog, and we raised him happily for 16 years before he died of old age in 2011.

The boys constantly pleaded with me to get a puppy and I kept refusing, but after I got back from Mexico, I agreed to go with them to the nearby animal shelter. We promised ourselves that this was just a courtesy visit, and that under no circumstances would we adopt a pet.

One rainy Saturday morning we went there and scouted the cages, looking at all the dogs waiting for adoption, and then we went to the second floor to look at the cats and kittens. My husband, who was allergic to cats, stayed outside while the boys and I went in and spent a delightful half-hour with the very energetic kittens who wanted to play and cuddle with us.

And then it happened – a tiny kitten with a black and white tuxedo pattern climbed into my lap and wouldn't leave me. My son begged me to take him home, but I reminded him that his dad was allergic. He wouldn't give up and went outside to get his father, to see if he would agree to play with the kitten a bit – maybe he wasn't allergic to this specific one?

My husband agreed, and after an hour in a room with the kitten, he confirmed that he really wasn't allergic to it.

As I said, I'm not a cat person and I had never had a cat, but we all fell in love with this little kitten who was so full of energy and love, and at the end of the day we caved and adopted Neo.

I raised Neo like he was a puppy. He even had a leash, and I would take him out on a walk in the neighborhood every day. I got him a toy bone, and every time I called his name, he would run to me and sit at my feet, waiting for a snack or a treat. We took Neo everywhere with us, to the grocery store, to the car wash, even when we went camping over the weekend. The neighbors all loved him and greeted him with treats when he snuck into their yards.

I remember when we couldn't find him one day and the whole neighborhood helped us search for him. When we called his name, we heard him meowing, but couldn't figure out where the sound was coming from. After a few minutes, when the meows got stronger, we realized they were coming from the neighbor's garage. We asked them to open their garage door, and as soon as the door was lifted, Neo came out, ran straight into my arms and licked my lips in gratitude, like an actual dog!

Neo was a very special cat. My father, who was captivated by his unique beauty, drew a picture of Neo and sent it over from Israel for my sons to hang up in their room.

Words can't explain the bond I had with Neo. All those nights I sat in front of the fireplace weeping for my failed marriage, he sat by my side, licking my tears away, trying to comfort me in those moments when I felt more alone than ever before.

When we adopted Neo, he was only four weeks old and, like any kitten of that age, had a healthy appetite and in a short time doubled his weight, growing to be a beautiful tuxedo cat. But after a few months we noticed a sudden change in his mood and behavior. After a while, he stopped eating and lost much of the weight he had gained.

When he was six months old, all the vets had given up and told me there was nothing they could do to save him, but something inside of me couldn't accept that he was beyond help. I fed him with a syringe three times a day, trying to save his life by helping him gain weight again.

I did this for three months until at last, on May 28th, 2015, when Neo could no longer keep any food down, the hospital said I should put him to sleep and end his misery.

I don't know if cats can cry, but when we said farewell, a tear dropped from my eye and also from his.

The four of us were sitting in the car, sobbing, finding it hard to believe that Neo passed away at only nine months old.

Suddenly my phone rang and when I saw it was the hospital calling, I answered. It was the vet who did the autopsy I had requested for Neo to find out what was wrong with him.

"Neo was born with a disease called FIV (feline immunodeficiency virus), which is, unfortunately, common among kittens, and they usually die from it within a few weeks of their birth," she explained.

"The fact that Neo lasted that long is very unusual... He must have loved you very much," she added, "because according to what I see inside his stomach, he has been clinically dead for a long time now, and he kept on living just for you. You did the right thing putting him to sleep today. It's a miracle that he was alive for so many months."

I will never forget that day. It was the Friday of Memorial Day weekend, and when we got home my husband suggested we go on a trip instead of staying at home grieving for our dead cat. The boys and I were so sad we didn't want to go anywhere, and my husband got angry, packed a bag and took off in our SUV, leaving us alone for the entire long weekend.

I cried for that cat like I had never cried before, not even for my dog Skip, who I raised for 16 years, and I asked myself, why is he running away again when things get difficult?

At that moment I knew that it wasn't only the cat that died. My marriage was dead and had been for a long time.

Chapter 16: This Time, I'm Leaving

I'D LIKE TO BELIEVE that everyone in our lives has a role to play, and Neo definitely played a very important role in mine. Neo taught me the most important lesson of all – To let go!

It was the children's summer vacation, and my husband suggested that he take them to Israel for the first two weeks of summer, leave them at their grandparents' for a few weeks, and then I would join them for the last two weeks, and bring them back home in time for school.

And so, on July 3rd, 2015, my husband and the boys took a flight to Israel, and I was left behind with a very clear plan. That plan had been forming in my mind ever since he came up with the brilliant idea of removing the kids from the scene by taking them to Israel.

As soon as I got back from the airport, I started calling local real estate agents, looking for a house to rent. I was amazed at how quickly I managed to find my dream house. After only two days of searching, I found a lovely house in nearby Foster City, completely furnished and stocked, down to towels and bed linen.

Later I found out that it belonged to a divorced woman who lived there by herself and designed it very tastefully, with varied art pieces that created a calm, peaceful atmosphere.

The real estate agent told me that the owner was moving on to the next chapter in her life and was looking for someone to take good care of the house and its contents.

The rent was somewhat higher than the market value, in part because the owner wanted to find a relatively wealthy and trustworthy tenant. At first, when I heard how selective the owner was, I doubted that she would let me and my twin boys rent the place, but after she heard my story, she agreed to let me live there, and accepted my application.

Wasting no time, I signed the lease, and on July 10th got the keys to the house.

I decided that this time I would not be the one who was being abandoned, but rather the one who leaves! And so, I packed my clothes and shoes, as well as the boys'. Apart from my father's paintings, the coffee machine and the vacuum cleaner, I took nothing from the house.

I managed the move by myself, and bit by bit I set up this new home, which soon became my sanctuary.

I will never forget my first night in my new home. After a long day of-cleaning and unpacking, I went for a swim in the nearby college Olympic pool. It was late at night and I was the only one there. The pool seemed to invite me in for a cleansing and liberating swim. Swimming to the light of the moon, lap by lap, powering through the water current, I felt like I was shedding the enormous baggage I had been carrying for years.

Two weeks to the day they had left for Israel, my husband landed in San Francisco very late at night. And just as he expected, I came to pick him up from the airport. When we got home, he unloaded his bags and headed for the front door. I stayed in the car.

A few minutes later, after he noticed that I was lingering in the car, he came out and asked why I wasn't coming in. I took a deep breath and looked straight into his eyes.

"I don't live here anymore," I said.

My husband stared at me. "I don't understand," he said.

"I rented a house in Foster City for me and the boys," I replied. "I moved out, and when I get back from Israel with the boys, we will sit them down and tell them together that we are getting a divorce."

As I was driving away, my husband was still standing there, a look of shock on his face.

"Wow! That felt *so* good!!" I exclaimed as I drove to my new home.

It felt good to be strong and steady, and not break in front of him. It felt good to be independent, and not need his help or his presence. It felt good not to be abandoned again, and to take control over my life!

My trip to Israel a few weeks later was not easy, mainly because I had to conceal the big news from everyone, but I promised myself not to ruin the boys' vacation, and to wait until we returned to San Francisco. Then we would sit them down and tell them together.

Our visit to Israel went by quickly, as all good things do. Soon, we said goodbye to everyone and took a long flight back to San Francisco.

My husband, who was waiting for us at the airport and had missed the boys very much, greeted them with a big hug. I made sure I stayed detached and reserved, and tried to hurry everyone home. I picked up our bags and headed for the parking lot where my husband had parked his car.

After we got home and I helped them unpack, the four of us sat down in the living room to break the news – that mom and dad were getting a divorce.

To my great relief, they took it quite well and didn't seem at all surprised.

My younger son asked, "Dad, if mom would be in the hospital, like you were, would you take care of her like she took care of you?"

We were both taken aback by his direct question, but my husband replied at once, "Of course. I will always take care of mom."

Chapter 17: Saving Myself from Myself

THE NEXT CHAPTER of my life was full of revelations.

The boys loved the new house in Foster City. That made the move much easier for me, as did knowing that during the weeks they spent with their dad, they were staying in their old familiar bedrooms, unlike the other times he had left home and rented a crummy, one-bedroom apartment.

This time, they would stay one week with me in a big beautiful house, filled with everything they could want, and then back to their own familiar spacious house to spend the following week with their dad.

The boys loved the new neighborhood and made a lot of new friends. The welcoming environment gave them confidence and independence, and when they finished 7th grade at their old school, they asked that we transfer them to the school near our house in Foster City for 8th grade before they headed to high school.

I must admit that at first, being alone was very hard for me. Every week I didn't have the kids was insufferable. I felt lost and isolated and tried to fill my evenings with activities – yoga, swimming, shopping, work; anything that would keep me from sitting at home alone.

I remember in those days I called every girlfriend within a hundred miles to see whether she was available to meet me, but most of them were busy with their own families, which only added sorrow and self-pity to my already melancholy mood.

I tried not to hang onto the kids, but to take strength from the fact that I was a single mother, providing for her family and marching forward through the next chapter in her life.

Being separate from my husband was also hard at first, and I sometimes felt lonesome in that big bed, but deep down I knew that sharing a bed with someone who had been such a stranger to me all these years actually meant that I had already been alone.

Nothing is worse than being alone in a relationship, and loneliness was far better than rejection and humiliation.

The new home that became my sanctuary – a "nest for the soul" as my therapist called it – played a major role in my recovery, and served as a passageway to a safe, new place where I could be myself completely and heal my broken heart, which was still bleeding.

During that time, many things were revealed to me in a brand-new light.

I discovered, for instance, that for years my husband had been visiting countless matching websites, looking for relationships with other women. I also discovered that being alone was not so bad, and the thing I feared the most turned out to be quite wonderful.

A few other nasty surprises presented themselves to me during this transition period.

When my husband and the boys were away for summer vacation in Israel, a good friend of mine came to visit with her young daughter. We had been friends since before the kids were born. It was a lovely summer evening, which means it was cold, due in large part to San Francisco's position between the ocean and the Central Valley, which makes for cold summer nights, and warm winter days, as opposed to the rest of the state.

We were sitting next to the outdoor fireplace, under the stars, laughing about life and telling each other our deepest secrets. Her daughter was watching TV inside and asked if she could have some popcorn. As soon as I jumped up to go make it, my friend got up and said she would do it.

I was happy that she didn't feel like a guest in my house and was comfortable finding her way around my kitchen. After a while, when she hadn't returned, I went back inside the house to see if she needed help. I couldn't believe what I saw – my "friend" was going through my purse! Her hand was deep inside my purse, searching for something...

As soon as she noticed me, she froze, and right away called her daughter, saying it was late, and they needed to go.

At that moment, dozens of pennies dropped, and all the lightbulbs came on in my head. I was horrified by what had just happened.

I bet you're wondering, what is she talking about? What happened?

So, let me tell you.

More than once over the last few years, friends who came to our home on weekends and holidays would complain that cash had disappeared from their purses while they were staying at our house. One even went so far as to blame one of my sons for stealing $300 from her purse. Of course, it was quickly asserted that there was no way in hell our boys would touch a single dollar of someone else's money, but still, it remained a mystery.

Sometimes, when cash disappeared from my wallet inside purse, I just assumed that my husband took it, and vice versa. For years we couldn't solve the mystery, but on that day when I found my friend going through my purse, everything became clear.

I haven't spoken to her since, and to this day I don't know what became of her.

That was the first time I lost a good friend. It never occurred to me that for years she was stealing money from me and my guests.

An additional unpleasant revelation occurred when I was having a nice dinner in San Francisco with another friend of many years. She confessed that while I was living in Israel, she and another friend met with my husband to try and convince him to end his affair with the young art student.

I remember almost choking on my food when she told me how they used to go out with my husband and his girlfriend while I was living in Israel.

I quickly ended my relationship with her as well.

Yes, this was my spring cleaning.

I got rid of all those friends who weren't really friends, so that I could start a clean slate.

It was Yom Kippur, and for the first time in my life, at 43 years old, I found myself alone on this special and holy day. My husband picked up the boys before sundown, so I even had to eat the last meal by myself.

When the fast started, I withdrew into myself and decided that I would not dwell in self-pity, but rather take this day to reflect and sit with all the painful memories. To connect to all those parts of me I wasn't so proud of, to forgive myself for all those years I emotionally panhandled from everyone around me, mainly from my husband.

I dreaded that day. I was worried it would be so hard for me to be alone. Alone, with no family, with no husband, with no home. Alone!

The synagogue was my sanctuary on the Eve of Yom Kippur, and even though I felt like a stranger there, it was wonderful and uplifting to sing in unison with everyone, to pray together, to look inward. I drew strength and great power from that experience, but most importantly – faith. Faith in myself. Faith that things would get better, that I would never really be alone, that I had the power to grow, to spread my wings and soar.

The next morning, I wrote the following in my journal:

"September 23ʳᵈ, 2015, the Day of Yom Kippur-

I woke up early this morning to a day of peace, cleansing and self-reflection. I always feared this day – how and when it would end – but for some reason this year I feel lighter... maybe because *he* is not here! The wounds are starting to heal, and the scars are beginning to fade. But most importantly, it is all about acceptance.

Acceptance can only happen when you make the decision to stop being ashamed, to respect myself, to see the beauty in everything, to look back without embellishing or making excuses.

On this Day of Yom Kippur, I know that it is my choice to feel like I am the victim, to hate, to be angry and resentful, or to feel courageous and free, open to, and anticipating the future.

On this Day of Yom Kippur, I choose to forgive myself, and I choose to believe that I can accomplish anything I set my mind to. I always swam against the current. I

must learn my lesson and start swimming
with the current and not against it."

When I finished writing, I sat in a lotus position on the living room floor, gazing out the windows and flipping through the Jewish textbook 'Tehillim' (**Psalms** – the poems and hymns of King David, in the original **Hebrew**) my good friend in Israel gave to me. At that moment, a small sparrow flew into the living room and landed beside me.

For a moment I froze, and then I smiled at the bird and said:

"I am never alone. Even this bird that came here to keep me company fills my heart with light and love."

Later that year, I celebrated finalizing my divorce with a friend who visited from Israel at the end of December. We spent an exciting week together, going up to Napa Valley, site-seeing, and spending New Years' Eve in Las Vegas, capped off by a Maroon 5 concert and fireworks at midnight.

We were watching the fireworks at midnight, and I stood there, feeling happy for every couple kissing around me.

For the first time in my life, I didn't feel jealous or lonely. On the contrary – I felt safe, enlightened. Whole.

I had saved myself from myself.

Chapter 18: Not Your Typical American Girl

WHEN I FIRST CAME to America 16 years ago, with broken English and a big ego, it dawned on me that it would take years to bridge the gap between myself and the natives, whose mother tongue is English, and whose culture was vastly different than my own.

Over the years I managed to improve my communication skills. I also made an effort to improve my accent, but I always sounded different, which did not play to my advantage in my current position in the firm.

Status was important among my peers, which led me to believe that it might be better to hide the fact of my divorce. I let everyone assume that I was still married with two kids and a dog, living in a beautiful house with picket fences.

No one at work had any idea what was going on in my private life.

I must admit that for a long time I also perceived divorce as a kind of curse, and for the first few years I couldn't even utter that word, so I just lied.

In order to move forward in my career and pursue a partnership path at the firm, I was asked to work with an executive coach on my communication skills, as well as a speech coach to improve my pitch and accent.

The initial feedback I got from the executive coach, who I adore to this day, was rather unpleasant and focused on two main aspects: my appearance and my form of expression.

She explained to me the importance of perception – perception is reality. She also explained that the average American male, listening to my high-pitched voice and my strange accent, would find it difficult to concentrate on the content of my conversation, let alone take me seriously.

I tried not to take any of this personally, and I agreed to work with the two coaches who were appointed by the firm for a period of 18 months.

At first, I was asked to change my image – my appearance and my tone of voice. I changed the way I dressed, the way I wore my hair, and practiced a slower, deeper speaking voice.

Over time, the change became more and more noticeable, and some days I didn't even recognize myself in the mirror, wearing all these masks.

But the hardest thing to do was work on my accent reduction with the dialect coach. Our weekly sessions took up most of my time and became my nightmare. In these sessions, I had to work on the position of my jaw and the rolling of my tongue, trying to pronounce every sound and syllable correctly. For a moment I felt like Eliza Doolittle from *My Fair Lady* – a Cockney flower girl with a thick, unintelligible accent, who is taken in and given speech lessons by Professor Henry Higgins, a phonetician, in an attempt to pass her off as a lady.

After months of hard work and hours of practice, I managed to improve my accent and my speech, but despite the compliments I received from colleagues, and my close friends who noticed the improvement, I was still frustrated by the gap that seemed as if it would never be closed.

Dealing with my new status as a divorcee while trying to adapt to my surroundings rather than be who I really was only intensified my feelings of inferiority and damaged my self-image in a way that made me feel lost and alone among my colleagues.

Come spring, the list of new partners was posted, and to my disappointment I was not promoted that year.

In time I would learn the truth of the saying "Rejection is God's Protection," and that although I did not get the thing I wished for and wanted so much, eventually it set me free.

That year, I held the Passover Seder (the celebratory dinner on Passover Eve) at my house with all of my friends.

Reading from the *Haggadah*, the old Jewish tale about the Hebrews' journey from slavery to freedom and that first Passover felt symbolic to me in so many ways – I also celebrated my own freedom.

I came to accept that it might be better to be authentic – to be who I really am, and not someone who I am not.

Chapter 19: Love it or List it

LOVE IT OR LIST IT is my favorite reality show on HDTV. I used to watch it every night after the boys went to bed. It's always entertaining to watch the competition between the real estate broker who tries to convince the couple to sell their house and buy a new one, and the interior designer who meanwhile remodels the current home into their "dream home" and tries to convince the couple to remain.

If only I had known that one day I would be faced with the very same dilemma…

In November 2016, my ex-husband informed me that he could no longer afford to keep the house and would therefore be moving to a smaller rented apartment in a less expensive area.

Within a few weeks, I found myself collapsing under the weight of both the rent on my house in Foster City and the mortgage payments on the house my ex-husband abandoned. Paying the bank as well as my landlord was way beyond my budget, and my savings were being depleted.

I had to make a decision, and fast – whether to sell the house and pay off the mortgage, or to move back into our old house and stop paying the monthly rent in our lavish house in Foster City.

I remember the day I walked into the house after my ex-husband left and cleared out his stuff. The walls were cracked everywhere, mold and dirt in every corner, and a stench like something had crawled into a hole in the wall and died.

As I walked into the bedroom, chills went down my spine and I felt suffocated as I scanned the room, thinking, if only these walls could talk...

I asked one of the contractors I knew to meet me at the house so I could get a cost estimate for the renovation. It was clear that, either way, I couldn't sell the house as it was, and if I wanted to get a good price for it, I would have to fix it up and upgrade it into a warm and inviting home.

I thought honesty was the best idea here and related the entire story to the contractor. He asked if I was sure I wanted to sell the house. When I explained why it was difficult for me to live there again, he suggested a compromise:

"Why don't you tell me how you would want the place to look, and at the end of the renovation, if you don't like it, you can put it up for sale."

"Wait, it's like *Love it or List it*!" I said, "But where will I get the money for an interior designer and a huge renovation?"

"Why don't you take out a loan?" he suggested.

And then it hit me, if the contractor was willing to wait until after the renovation was complete to be paid, maybe I would be able to get an appraisal from the bank after the renovation. If the estimation was high enough, maybe the bank would agree to give me a bigger mortgage.

It was a really great idea, but the question remained: would the contractor be willing to take that chance with me? After all, I could always sell the house at any point and pay him from what I had left after paying off the mortgage.

We agreed to sleep on it, and fortunately, the next morning the contractor accepted my offer.

I have to admit, I was skeptical at first. I never really believed I could fall back in love with my house like they do in that reality show. After all, that house held so many bad memories and bitter feelings for me.

Even so, I enjoyed being the interior decorator – choosing tiles, hardwood floors, the color of the walls, bedroom carpets, designing the state-of-the-art kitchen, and the ensuite bathroom for the master bedroom.

I was so busy with the house, I lost track of time, and just as the contractor promised, it was ready at the end of February.

After I redesigned the garden and gave it a thorough cleaning, I invited the appraiser from the bank.

I remember praying that the estimated value was high enough for me to refinance and buy my ex-husband's share of the house. I prayed for a miracle!

Yes, I believe in miracles! More than anything, I believe that good things happen to good people, and that people who are themselves generous will receive generosity in return. And that day, I received a blessing!

The estimated value of the house was so much higher than I had expected. I had enough to pay the contractor, and to buy my ex-husband's share from him.

Yes, eventually I fell in love with my house again. Like they say in my favorite show: I decided to love it!

The first night I spent there, before I fell asleep, I wrote in my journal:

> "11 p.m. After a refreshing shower, I am lying in my huge bed, the new bed I got for myself. It's good to be home. There is a sense of calm and security here. I have built a sanctuary for myself. A sanctuary for my heart and my soul. A place I can call HOME!
>
> I wish this home was in Israel, near everyone, but we are here. And here, in this moment, we are forging our future and living our lives.

I love that nothing in this house brings up sad memories or bad feelings for me. On the contrary – it gives me strength, hope, a sense of fulfillment, renewal and a new chapter!

Our lovely neighbors, who are like family to us, have missed us so much, they welcomed us with cake and flowers and a loving embrace.

Everything feels so right, so good, so wonderful, I couldn't have asked for more in any way. It's absolutely perfect!!

Goodnight, in my new home."

March 20th, 2017

Chapter 20: Sky the Rescue Dog

ONE OF THE THINGS I promised the boys before we moved back into our house was that this time we could adopt a kitten or a puppy. We weren't allowed to have pets in the house we rented in Foster City, but now in our own house, we could do as we pleased.

Promises should be kept, and so, on the first Saturday after we moved, we went to the nearby animal shelter to see whether they had any kittens or puppies that were looking for a home.

The boys couldn't agree on whether they wanted a cat or a dog and tried to convince me to take both. When they understood we wouldn't be able to take home two pets on the same day, and that we should start with one, they decided on a kitten.

We went up to the second floor, where we had found our beloved Neo two years before, and scanned every cage looking for a kitten, but we only saw more mature cats.

We were really keen on adopting a tiny kitten, and when we couldn't find any, we headed out, disappointed.

On our way out one of my sons asked: "Mom, can we maybe look at the dogs? I know we said we were going to get a cat, but can we just take a look? Please?"

I couldn't refuse him, and so we went back inside and walked around the first floor, looking at cages that were filled with countless dogs and puppies looking for a home.

It broke my heart to see them, and all I wanted was to get out of there as quickly as I could, before I changed my mind and took one of them home with us.

Suddenly, my son stopped in front of one of the cages and called out for me to come see. It was a dog named Rosie and she had one brown eye and one blue eye.

Without much interest, I looked at the dog and, seeing her different color eyes, said, "Her eyes look weird, like she was born defected."

My son was hurt by my reaction and asked me to look again.

"Mom, look how special she is."

I turned back to take another look and the moment our eyes met my heart trembled to see this two-year-old abandoned dog looking into my eyes with such sadness.

At that moment the adoption counselor came over and asked if I wanted to go inside Rosie's room to get to know her better, and without thinking twice about it I said, "Yes."

I went into Rosie's room and she greeted me, overjoyed and enthusiastic. I asked her to sit in Hebrew, and she immediately sat down, looking straight into my eyes and smiling broadly.

"Give me your hand Rosie," I said in Hebrew, and she gave me her paw.

"Give me a kiss," I said in Hebrew, and she immediately gave me a kiss on the lips.

"Wow!!" I said. "She understood everything I said to her in Hebrew!"

And suddenly I noticed how amazingly beautiful this mixed husky named Rosie was.

"Who left this gorgeous dog here?" I asked the counselor, "Who could have given her up? How could anyone leave her?"

"Let me look in her file," she said, and went to the office to open Rosie's file.

When she came back with the file, she said, "It says here that Rosie is aggressive towards men."

"Great!" I smiled, "I'm taking her home with me!"

And so, on Saturday, March 25th, 2017, we adopted a dog and, excited as can be, introduced her to her new home.

What a gift we were given that day! A real treasure. Rosie is an obedient and noble dog, with a look in her eyes that goes straight to the heart. She reminded me of my brother's dog, Sky.

I didn't like the name Rosie. It reminded me of an old lady, whereas Rosie the dog was full of energy, like a puppy. I was looking for a new name for our new dog, and so I gave my brother a call to see what he thought. I showed him a picture of Rosie.

"Doesn't she look just like Sky?"

"Yes," my brother agreed immediately, "she has the same exact look in her eyes."

"Would it be ok with you if I called her Sky?"

"She's your dog. You can give her any name you like."

I was relieved when my brother gave his consent, and from that day to this, Sky has filled our home with warmth and love, charming everyone with her unique eyes – one brown and one blue, like the blue sky.

The boys forgot all about the kitten they wanted to adopt, and Sky became their pride and joy. At night she would sleep in their beds – alternating, one night with one and the next with the other (she continues that practice today), and every morning, upon rising to start their day, they would first give her a big hug.

A couple of days after we'd adopted Sky I wrote in my journal:

"March 27th, 2017

It has been a week since we moved back here, and even though I didn't get much sleep the last couple of nights, I'm filled with positive energy – flowing and succeeding, conquering and making dreams come true – and Sky is one of those dreams. What a picture-perfect dog! She's only been with us two days and already she's an inseparable part of the family. It's so much fun! Yes, it's a huge responsibility and it takes a lot of courage and a lot of money that I don't have right now, but I feel like it's the most amazing thing I've done for myself and the boys. What a huge love! It really is a dream come true...

Good Night."

Even though we adopted Sky (AKA 'Rosie') when she was two years old, it took her no time at all to learn her new name and respond to it when we called her. Just as quickly, she learned the rules of the house, and followed my lead (yes, I am the Alpha). Every night we would take her to her favorite dog park, where she would run and play with her friends.

One night, right before it got dark, Sky and I were at that dog park, which was empty but for the two of us.

While we sat, taking a break after playing "fetch" before heading home, the gate suddenly opened and a couple came in with their dog, who was the spitting image of Sky.

Struck by how similar the two dogs were, I asked the couple the age of their dog.

"Kelly is two years old," they said.

We were all smiling, looking at the two dogs playing so nicely together.

I asked when they adopted her, and they shared that they bought her when she was a few months old from a family whose dog had a litter of six.

The woman took out her cellphone and showed me pictures of their dog Kelly when she was a puppy, as well as the mother – a huge brown-eyed Pitbull that reminded me of Sky, and the father – a miniature husky with piercing blue eyes, just like Sky's.

When I asked for Kelly's date of birth, and they said, "February 9th, 2015," it was clear beyond doubt – Sky and Kelly were sisters!

"Do you recall if they also had a puppy like my Sky when you picked up Kelly?" I asked, and then corrected myself – "I mean Rosie?"

They both looked at me, confused, and then looked again at the pictures they took that day, when suddenly the woman exclaimed, "Yes! There was another family there, they bought Rosie, and so Kelly was the only one left!"

This was truly an incredible coincidence! They were not even from the area; they were just passing through with their dog Kelly, who turned out to be Sky's sister, and decided to go into the dog park just as me and Sky were playing there! What a touching reunion.

The love between the two sisters who must have missed each other so much, the chemistry between them as they played, resonated so deeply with all of us, and we stayed there for hours, even though it had gotten dark, excited by this chance meeting. We kept taking pictures, documenting every moment of this wonder, so we would remember the magical evening.

Ever since that day, whenever someone asks me about Sky's different colored eyes, I smile broadly and say: "Sky gets the brown eye from her mother and the blue eye from her father."

Chapter 21: There's a First Time for Everything

IF SOMEONE WOULD HAVE told me 20 years ago that I wouldn't be living in Israel, but in the States, and that I wouldn't be married, but divorced, and have twin boys who I raise in a foreign country, I probably would have told them they were crazy. But this is the reality. I guess life is full of surprises.

The journey into the unknown took me to the edge, physically and mentally, and now I was experiencing many things for the very first time as a single woman. After 28 years in a relationship, married for almost 20 of those years, I was single again.

I experienced moments and situations it had never occurred to me that I would find myself in, let alone enjoy. For example, I always felt sorry for people dining alone at a restaurant, sitting by themselves at the bar or at a table for two.

Little did I know that the day would come when I would be dressing up for my first night out in the city, by myself.

Now this was a first for me. I had on my tight jeans, my white chiffon blouse, brown boots and a matching leather jacket. San Francisco, here I come...

It was Saturday night and the atmosphere was lively, restaurants and bars packed with people.

The restaurant I was heading to was always fully booked, and you usually had to make reservations months in advance, especially on a Saturday night. After a 30-minute wait, a place opened up at the bar. I sat down, a little embarrassed, and waved to the waiter for a menu.

When I pictured myself dining alone, it never occurred to me that the people sitting next to me would make my dinner anything but solitary. I soon realized that there were many others like me who came there to have dinner on their own, and were looking to start a conversation.

I met a lot of people that night,–some were tourists and some locals who were regulars at that restaurant.

After I paid the waiter, I said goodbye to everyone and headed home, pleased with myself for going out alone, and happy to find out that it wasn't that bad.

My next challenge was going to the movies by myself. Whenever I used to see people walking into a movie theatre by themselves, I would think it so sad that they had no one to go with.

I will never forget the first movie I watched by myself in the theatre. It was a Will Smith movie, *Collateral Beauty*. It was a great film with an emotional story. I cried my eyes out through most of it, but I also enjoyed the freedom and the courage of sitting in a movie theatre by myself, without worrying about what others may think. Just sitting there engrossed in what was happening on the screen.

Once again, I acknowledged that it wasn't that bad. As nice as it may be to go with friends, it was also liberating to know that I didn't need a companion if I wanted to go and enjoy a good movie on my own.

So far, I dared to go to a restaurant and to a movie by myself, but the thought of traveling alone still made me bitterly sad.

My hairdresser here in California used to tell me about her world travels, and I remember being so jealous of her courage. I was always impressed by the fact that she wasn't afraid to travel alone, and even enjoyed it.

One day, while she was cutting my hair, I told her about a place I'd heard of – a pet-friendly resort in Mendocino, a small town four hours north of San Francisco. The resort, which overlooks Mendocino Bay, serves vegan meals that are made using produce grown in the resort's historic eco farm. They also offer yoga classes for guests, and the best thing of all – not only are they dog-friendly, they actually treat dogs better than humans.

We were both curious to see what the place looked like. We browsed the internet and found their website, and in their gallery, we saw wide open fields and a breathtaking view of the ocean.

My hairdresser suggested I call them and see if they had an available room for me while the boys were away in Dallas with their dad.

It took me a moment to understand what she was talking about. Was she suggesting that I should go alone with Sky?

And then, without wasting any time, I called and booked a room with an ocean view for two nights for me and Sky.

Just like that, complete spontaneity.

The drive up to Mendocino was one of the most beautiful drives I've ever taken, with breathtaking views. The road that headed west left me astonished; 12 miles into the thick of majestic redwoods, and then you pop out at the ocean, with the trees towering on both sides of the road, their tops touching, like they were hugging each other above us.

The combination of Sky – who was silent the entire ride – and the music I had chosen for the drive had me feeling peaceful and safe until we reached our destination. When we entered the resort, we were greeted with warm smiles and kind words, and led to our beautiful suit overlooking the ocean.

Even though I was the only guest there who was traveling without a human companion, and a few of the other guests asked me about it, I didn't feel bad, or lonely.

I took a walk on the beach with Sky every morning and rented a pet-friendly canoe designed for both humans and dogs to explore the beautiful Big River. I felt so lucky and so happy, grateful for the privilege to experience this wonderful time with my beloved dog.

We returned home, both of us filled with new experiences and good energies, and as I was unpacking my bag, I started to plan my next trip with her.

Chapter 22: Yoga School

THE FIRST TIME I practiced yoga, I was eight months pregnant, with a huge belly and legs like a hippopotamus from the amount of water I retained. I remember how heavy and clumsy I felt. All I wanted was some form of physical activity that would be conducive with my situation.

It was way back when all we had were video tapes, and I was able to find a "Yoga for Pregnant Women" video (VHS) tape in the public library. It became my favorite exercise tape, and so I ended up renting it for a whole month, practicing the same lesson every day.

That routine exercise, especially the breathing and the relaxation, helped me get through the last month of my pregnancy with a sense of calm and optimism.

My second taste of yoga, as you may recall, was when I lived in Israel with the boys. My private yoga teacher in Tel Aviv, who came to my apartment every week to teach me the basics of yoga, made me promise that when I returned to San Francisco, I would continue to practice my yoga.

And so, I did.

I kept that promise like I would a sacred vow, and every Saturday morning I practiced yoga in my favorite studio in downtown San Francisco. The studio became my second home and my new family.

Months passed, and my appetite to learn more about the yoga philosophy grew. The deeper I went into my practice, the bigger my yearning was to know even more, and a new dream started to form – to enroll in a yoga teacher training program.

Unfortunately, my husband didn't approve of it at all. In fact, he objected outright, and without his support, as a mom of two, that newfound dream quickly dissipated.

I remember my disappointment when I had to inform my yoga teacher that my husband wasn't willing to support me or help me with the kids so that I could find time for the training program.

"Don't worry," she said, "this probably isn't the right time for you. Your time will come. I promise."

I remember thinking, what could she mean by that? If not now, then when? I was turning 40, and most of the students in the program were in their twenties.

Little did I know that one day I would be on my own, free to do as I pleased. And, just as she promised, my time came, five years later.

Today, I know this to be true – there is a time for everything.

When I was still married, I was neither mature enough nor receptive enough to go through the transformation I went through in yoga school.

School started in September 2017, and on the very first day I recognized that it was going to be a difficult and challenging journey for me, and that in order to succeed in the program, I would have to focus on the here and now without thinking about tomorrow.

As a single mother of two with a fulltime job, I knew I would have to work twice as hard and use every available minute if I wanted to keep up with my classmates. And so, I rose early every morning to practice and get a head start before classes begin, and at night I would stay up late to finish most of my homework.

On the first day, we were asked to practice in silence so that we could tune in to our emotions and physical sensations. I loved the silence. It was an invitation to be with myself and fully connect to what I was experiencing at that moment.

On the fourth day, my body was already aching, and my muscles were tight. I had pain in my back, my legs, my thighs. My body felt as heavy as a rock, but I realized that there was much more pain in store for me, emotional as well as physical, in this journey that had just begun.

Aside from classes and projects, we also had to practice yoga every day, and choose one or two things in our lives that we were willing to give up. It had to be something we were dependent on, maybe even addicted to. In giving it up we were devoting ourselves to the transformational process.

After giving it much consideration, I decided to make several changes in my life – to give up coffee and alcohol and to maintain a vegan diet.

To be honest, I used to drink five espressos a day and my coffee machine was overworked. I was so addicted to coffee; I could drink a double espresso in the middle of the night and go to sleep right after.

It was a huge sacrifice and a drastic change for me, but after a few weeks, when my body cleansed itself, I felt much more balanced and alert to everything around me.

A few weeks into the school year I met my beloved teacher of Bhakti Yoga, which is a spiritual path or spiritual practice within Hinduism. Bhakti is an expression of devotional love.

The first time she taught us, we were asked to write a few words about what God meant to us and what caused us to take this difficult journey in search of truth.

When we were done writing, each of us sat down with the teacher privately, so we could talk about what we wrote, and she could get to know us better.

When it was my turn, she asked that I tell her the one thing I wanted or desired for myself.

I paused to think, and then replied, "I want to heal."

I told her about myself in a few words, and she handed me a necklace with 108 beads.

"This will be your Mala," she said. "Every night before you go to bed, I want you to say 'Hari Om' 108 times."

"Hari" in Sanskrit means "remover," and it refers to removing personal suffering, troubles, blockage, pain and subjugations. "Hari Om" in Sanskrit means "removing obstacles."

"How long should I do this for?"

"Forty consecutive days," she said.

She explained that in order to feel even the slightest form of change in our perceptions, we must do something persistently for 40 days straight. If for some reason we skip a day, we must start all over again, otherwise it will not have an effect.

9.16.2017 – Day 1:

"Tonight, I start 40 days of chanting – saying the 'Hari Om' mantra 108 times, and for the first time I am able to write down what I wish for. Peace of mind. I want to stop being afraid of being alone, I want to let go of the past and to find who I really am. I want to be authentic again, to soften, to open my heart. "

9.19.2017 – Day 4:
"This morning I felt wonderful getting up before sunrise and practicing yoga, especially for the upcoming Rosh Hashana (Jewish New Year), a time of cleansing and renewal. This time, the feeling of renewed strength comes from the inside rather than from the outside, which is in itself an amazing accomplishment. Happy New Year to me…"

9.27.2017 – Day 12:
"Twelve is the day of my birth; 12 women in my yoga class; 12 days of keeping up this mantra tradition by saying 'Hari Om' 108 times, without knowing what it will do. I'm just experimenting, curious to see how, and if, it will affect me. I am trying to give in to the process, to see where it will take me, how much it will open me up to a brand-new world. To connect to my inner self, to be authentic and to not be afraid! Not be afraid! Not be afraid!"

9.30.2017 – Day 15:
"Today I learned how Bhakti Yoga pierces right through to my soul. The question – who am I really? – excites me and scares the hell out of me. Do we accept who we really are, or do we try to be someone else?

Today was full of revelations. We learned different breathing techniques–pranayama

–and it is astonishing that we can actually create more space for air to come in by expanding the diaphragm. We can change the way we think, even the way we are perceived by others, all through breathing! Our energy, our thoughts, all of it is affected by breathing and by the way we hold air inside."

10.2.2017 – Day 17:
"Slowly, time is taking its course, and with time I realize that there is nothing like silence. I come to appreciate the strength within me and trust myself more and more... slowly... peacefully. It is quiet in my head; it is quiet inside of me. I like that it's so quiet; such peace cannot be explained. A moment without doubt or guilt, a moment without longing, a moment without worry, a moment without memories. A moment without regret or the feeling of missing out. A moment of here and now. A wonderful moment. Good night."

10.4.2017 – Day 19:
"I'm so sick of this pain that always comes when I sit down in bed. I hope it will go away the same way it came, or maybe it's just part of this journey. Sometimes it is exhausting and painful, and other times it is full of new discoveries, insights and new ways of thinking. Every day I get to know

myself more. My mother always used to say to me when I was a little girl – 'remember, there will always be those who will love you and those who will hate you'. Now, more than ever, this resonates with me."

10.15.2017 – Day 30:
"I'm not sure I am able to be completely devoted to this journey, but I try to stay within the lines and borders I drew for myself and to be in the moment. I try not to think of the near future, or the far future. I'm not always successful. Especially when my mind wanders and fears rise up and threaten to overpower me. In those moments, it always helps me to put my attention back on my breathing. It helps me to refocus on the here and now. The now, the present, can be so wonderful, especially if I learn to feel grateful for everything that I already have, if I don't fake it, if I stop thinking about everyone else and what they have and how far they got to in their lives; How they have so much and I am alone, in the dark, lost..."

10.17.2017 – Day 32:
"More than 30 days have passed, and I'm still not sure what is really going on with me. Is there any change happening in me? Enlightenment, openness, anything?? I will keep going until I see or find a way to

believe. I want to learn, and I crave to find out more and more. I'm ready, I just have to be open to receive it all, whatever it may be."

10.25.2017 – Day 40:
"Wow, I can't believe it's been 40 days since I started my nightly Japa ritual with 'Hari Om' as my mantra. I hope this is not the end, but the beginning of a long string of days and nights of concentration and persistence, peace of mind and transcendence. 'Hari Om', the sound of my voice comes out as an expression of freedom in my new life. Authenticity and respect for the things that are important and holy to me. That is what should be given priority in this spiritual journey in which I learn to connect to the 'self' and to who I really am.

This brings me back home to Israel, to my grandmother's house, to that little girl who had the strength and the courage to skip school and open her father's shoe store, to sell shoes while he was sitting 'Shiva' (the Jewish mourning period of seven days) for his father who had just passed away. To provide for my family, I opened that shoe store every day while everyone thought I was in school. When the 'Shiva' ended, I took a bus to my grandmother's house to give my father all the money I made selling the shoes.

Everyone was shocked at that 10-year-old girl's courage to run a shoe store by herself.

Yes, this was more than 30 years ago, but this is who I am!!!"

Chapter 23: The Accident

ONE NIGHT, AS I WAS driving on the highway to meet my classmates, a stone came flying out of the truck ahead of me, hit my front window and cracked the windshield glass on its right side. It sounded like a gunshot and scared me to death, and for a moment I thought the glass might shatter.

"Such bad luck" I thought. "I just bought this car…"

I hardly slept that night, thinking about what had happened and trying to figure out how to repair the damage to the glass.

The next morning, I called the insurance company to report the incident, to see if they will cover the damage and fix my window. I was worried that I wouldn't be able to pay for the repair, and I went into a long and exhausting argument over the phone with the insurance representatives.

I remember how hard I took it and how all of my energies were sucked into that one problem that at the time seemed like the end of the world.

That same morning, I decided that it wasn't safe to take my new car with the cracked front window and that I'd better take the old car to go into town. It was a Saturday morning and the roads were empty, except for several other drivers who were also taking the highway into San Francisco.

I was enjoying the drive and, since it was late evening in Israel, I called my Mom before they went to bed to see how they were doing.

While going 70 miles an hour I suddenly noticed that all the cars ahead of me were breaking and a string of cars started crashing into each other. Without making a sound I hit the brakes and heard the noise of shattered glass all around me.

My heart skipped a few beats, and all I could think of at that moment was that this was the end of me and that my mother on the other end of the line will have a stroke if she realizes there was an accident.

The car stopped. I opened my eyes and all around me, the cars that were involved in the accident were scattered on the highway with serious damage to their fronts, sides and backs. That moment felt like forever, but the strangest thing was that no one had hit me. My car was sitting in the middle of the road without a single dent or scratch.

"Is everything alright? Is everything alright??"

I suddenly heard my mother shouting on the other end of the line

For a moment I forgot she was there. I quickly came to my senses and answered her. My hands were shaking, and my heart was pounding, but I tried my best to get my mother to calm down. She stayed on the line with me until I got to school and when I got there, I let her speak to one of the teachers who assured her that I was completely fine.

When I hung up the phone, I burst into tears, my body shaking, as I held my teacher's hand. She hugged me and tried to calm me so I could explain what happened.

When I regained my strength, I told her about the dreadful multi-car accident and all the horrors I had seen driving through it. I kept crying when I told her that I didn't even stop to help anyone, I never left my car. Because I was so worried about my mom who was halfway across the world, I kept on driving until I got to the school.

"I don't understand!" I cried out, weeping, "How come nothing happened to me?? Everybody crashed into each other, and I was the only one who came out without a scratch? Why only me?"

My teacher leaned in and whispered in my ear, "This was probably not your time to leave."

She went on to say, "Someone up there is looking after you. We are thankful that nothing happened to you."

The rest of the day went by like in a dream. It hadn't sunk in yet that I was alive and that all of that really happened to me a few hours before.

When class was over, I turned on my cell and saw seven missed calls from my younger son.

I rushed outside and called him back to see what was wrong, and he picked up right away.

"Mom! Where are you? Why didn't you answer any of my calls??"

"I'm so sorry, you know we're not allowed to have cellphones in class. Is everything ok at home?"

He burst into tears. "Mom, I thought something had happened to you!! I heard on the news that there was a car accident on the highway coming into San Francisco, and I had a bad feeling that something had happened to you..."

I took a deep breath, apologized and calmed him down.

As soon as I got home, we all hugged, the boys and Sky and I, thankful for how lucky I had been.

That night, still in disbelief, I wrote in my journal:

> "Today changed my view and my perspective. For a moment I thought how pathetic it was to worry about that broken window in the morning, when I could have been killed in that horrifying accident on Route 101. Somebody up there wanted to give me a little perspective.
>
> Maybe that will strengthen my faith in how blessed and lucky I am.

Could it be that my grandmother is watching over me?"

Chapter 24: Graduation

TIME FLIES. It seemed like it yesterday that I started school, and now it was almost over.

The last few weeks of yoga school were intense. Each week we removed another layer, like peeling an onion. And each week we dug deeper into the core of our souls.

The physical and spiritual journey was full of insight, and my entire perspective changed. There were no shortcuts. In order to come out of my shell, I had to reconnect with all the different sides of me, even the ones I wasn't so proud of. The process of acceptance and the struggle with the ego – which has no place in the realm of yoga – allowed me to access areas in my body that were hitherto off limits.

Beyond the flexibility that I gained over time, my heart opened up, and the breath created space for a more mindful and conscious experience – in every movement, perception and action.

The philosophy of yoga has had a huge impact on my life. It changed my outlook on so many levels. I came to appreciate that yoga has many aspects aside from the physical ability and the breathing and meditation techniques.

For instance, Karma yoga, which is also known as Karma Marga, is the path of action without selfish motives. Doing good deeds is key to following this path, but the motivation is not any type of reward.

Part of our homework in Karma yoga was to take a weekend to volunteer for a cause of our choice. The idea of helping others was always appealing to me, and when my friends started coming up with ideas about where to volunteer for the weekend, I already knew the one thing I really wanted to do – feed the homeless.

San Francisco is known for the massive amount of homeless people crowding its streets. They lie on benches and sidewalks, seeking shelter from the freezing cold during the winter months.

When I brought this up with my group, they thought I had lost my mind.

"You're crazy! Those areas, where all the homeless people gather, are really dangerous!"

They unanimously rejected my idea, but I didn't lose hope, and decided to look for someone who would be willing to join me despite the risk. Happily, my Indian friend wasn't as fearful as the locals. She loved my idea and decided to join me on this mission.

The following Sunday I picked her up and we went to Costco for groceries, warm socks, blankets and beverages, and with a budget of a few hundred dollars managed to prepare 50 well-stocked packages.

That night, we loaded all the packages into two tactical backpacks and went roaming through the crowded streets to hand them out to the needy. At first, we hesitated to approach the ones who looked like they were mentally unstable or under the influence of drugs, but when we felt more secure and realized how grateful all of them were, we didn't discriminate, and gave a care package to every homeless person we met.

What a night!

Our legs were aching, and our backs were sore, carrying those heavy backpacks, but seeing all those people so happy and grateful for what they had been given filled our hearts with joy.

The beauty of giving to others and bringing them joy was definitely the highlight of our weekend and when we got home, we made a vow to get together every year during the holidays and hand out food and blankets to the homeless people in the streets of San Francisco.

Every year since then, we have continued that amazing experience of Karma yoga.

Having passed the practical exam of teaching a yoga class, my journey was almost at an end. The last thing that stood between me and my certificate was a 5-hour written test.

I studied every night, by myself or with my classmates, using every spare moment, but the amount of material I had to master in such a short time made me doubtful about my chances of passing the test. Still, I kept studying and focusing on my goal.

When the day of the exam arrived, I tried telling myself that if I managed to pass the CPA bar exam, I would manage to pass this as well. After a long day, I came home not quite sure how I did, but knowing that I did everything I possibly could – now it was out of my hands.

The next day I woke up all excited for the graduation ceremony. I was delighted that everyone could make it (except my family in Israel, of course), and that I would be able to celebrate this amazing accomplishment with my children and friends.

The highlight of the ceremony was when I was asked to deliver my speech. Standing in front of the audience and seeing my boys in the crowd was the most profound thing. There was nothing more exhilarating than seeing them looking so proud, appreciating the time and effort I had invested in order to get to this moment.

When I got off the stage, my teachers sprinkled me with rose petals, and my younger son, who couldn't wait, snatched the envelope out of my hand and went to open it. After a second he came running back.

"Mom!!" he shouted, "you passed the exam! You got 83!!!"

I was so relieved…

I passed! I got the certificate that allows me to teach yoga! I took the envelope from him and looked at my certificate. My eyes filled with tears.

Who would have thought I would become a yoga teacher at age 45??!!!

Chapter 25: Two Weeks of Bliss

TURNING A NEW PAGE. Life after yoga school seemed much more optimistic and peaceful. I was no longer obsessed with chasing the next thing, and for the first time in my life I recognized, what needs to happen will happen, no matter what, so I should flow with the changes rather than resist them. I must desist from the endless search for the next thing that will make me happy – the end of seeking is peace.

Happiness is always in me, and I alone have access to it. Only I can make myself happy or unhappy. Nothing in the world can take it away from me, unless I let it go myself.

All that was left for me to do was spread my wings and share this wonderful feeling with my loved ones. And so, I did. Two weeks after graduation, I bought three plane tickets, and the boys and I flew to Israel to surprise my dad for his 77th birthday.

We arrived on December 24th, four days before my father's birthday, for a 14-day trip; seven plus seven, like his age – 77.

Seeing my parents again, and the rest of our family who waited for us at the airport, was an exciting kick start to our two-week celebration.

Everywhere we went, we announced that it was my father's birthday, and in each place, we were welcomed, with warm greetings for the birthday boy.

That night I wrote in my journal:

"December 24th, 2017

We came to Israel for a visit. It's cold and wintery. It feels good to snuggle in bed and listen to the rain outside. The kids are already asleep, and I really hope they get over their jetlag soon.

Mom and Dad look great, and my sister is just an angel, with her big heart and her giving spirit. It's so good to see everyone, they're all so delightful, and I wish them many more magical moments like this one. A new perspective. Peace and tranquility. Absolute perfection.

I'm in a different place. A better place. A place of acceptance. A place of openness. A place of sensitivity and understanding. Of strength and power. A great place. "

On the eve of my Dad's birthday, I took him to one of the well-known fish restaurants on the beach. It was like when I was a young girl, going out with dad. We enjoyed a delicious meal while looking at the sunset and listening to the soft sound of the waves of the Mediterranean.

It was a wonderful evening with my darling father, who had always taught me to be in the here and now, and to enjoy every single moment we're given in this miraculous life.

The next morning, the entire family – my brother and his wife and kids, my sister and her husband and their children, my parents, the boys and I – went camping at the foot of Masada. Masada is one of the most popular attractions in Israel, an ancient stone fortress with a renowned history, located high above the Dead Sea on a tall, rocky mesa.

There, in the desert landscape, we celebrated my father's birthday with a festive dinner, presents and greetings. In the small hours of the night, we retired to our tents to sleep under a moonlit sky filled with countless stars.

The next morning, at dawn, we climbed to the top of the Masada Mountain in time to watch the sunrise. The view from the top left me astounded – eternal beauty, second to none in the world. There, in a fortress situated on top of an isolated rock in the middle of the Judean Desert, overlooking the Dead Sea, I decided to practice yoga and meditation.

On Tuesday the following week, I took my parents and my sons to Jerusalem. Tuesday – the day God called "twice as good" for travelling – was the perfect day to take a trip to Jerusalem. We started our trip at the crowded Mahane Yehuda market. We stopped at every stall, savoring the scents and enjoying the wide variety of food. For the boys, who had never seen anything like it, it was a fun experience. It made me happy to see them so free, willing to try everything.

Our next stop was the Western Wall ('HaKotel HaMa'aravi') which, to me, is the holiest place on earth.

My Dad took the boys to the men's section, and my Mom and I went to the women's section. Standing next to my mother in front of the massive limestone wall intensified my feeling of elation at being in the Holy City and moved me to tears.

When we came out after the prayer, I glanced over to the men's side and saw both my boys leaning their foreheads against those ancient stones, praying silently. It was a touching image that will be forever etched in my memory.

The cherry on top was our trip to Eilat with my entire family. Although it was winter, the sun was out every day, warming our hearts and even tempting us to take a dip in the cool water of the Red Sea.

Here, in the city of eternal sunshine, I continued my tradition of practicing yoga at sunrise, this time on the beach with the soft murmur of the waves and the first rays of sunshine touching my body.

Our two weeks of bliss came to an end on January 8th, and the boys and I flew back to San Francisco.

On the flight home, miles above the earth, I started planning my first yoga class, which was scheduled to take place a few weeks later. The themes for my class were courage, faith and most important – awakening!!

Dare to believe,
Dare to dream,
Dare to connect,
Dare to reach beyond; and
Dare to stay AWAKE!

Chapter 26: London

THE YEAR 2018 started with openness and courage to try new things, believing in myself and in endless possibility.

I taught my first ever yoga class, which was a great success, and to my surprise, the school principal chose me for an internship under her personal guidance. The internship was for a period of eight weeks, and during that time I was asked to teach a community class once a week. In addition, I participated in the principal's classes as an apprentice in order to improve my teaching skills and practice hand assist (help the students during her class).

The opportunity to intern with one of the best, most famous yoga teachers in the world was a dream come true for me.

When I enrolled in yoga school, I had no intention of teaching. My main goal was to delve into it and learn as much as I could, but after teaching my first class, I was hooked. It was a wonderful feeling – the ability to connect with people and to help them find their balance and their ground in this dynamic world we live in – and I wanted to experience more of the same.

I cannot describe the happiness of observing people come into my class frantic and agitated, and see them find some calm and balance during practice.

My internship did a great deal for me in terms of becoming more professional and building my confidence as a teacher, but my main endeavor was to find my authenticity, without imitating or copying anyone, without being somebody I'm not. This important insight was definitely the selling point for me to keep teaching. I found a field in which I don't have to wear any masks or pretend to be anything I'm not. I could just be who I am, for better or worse, with my accent, with my directness, with my endless will to give, with the mistakes I make. Just be myself and speak my truth!!

The gift was so enormous, I wanted to share it with the world. I decided to teach pro bono, and to volunteer in any institute or any place that needed a yoga teacher. In my spare time, on evenings and weekends, I taught in a variety of places to diverse groups of people – battered women's shelter, teenage swim team, new mothers, girls' volleyball team, and even my colleagues at the office every Friday.

Everywhere, I managed to touch people, open them up to the wonders of yoga, and change their perspective.

There is a famous saying: "If you practice yoga once a week, it will change your mind. If you practice twice a week, it will change your body. But if you practice yoga every day, it will change your life." This proved to be absolutely true not only in my life, but also in the lives of my students.

Teaching hundreds of lessons recharged my batteries and inspired me to continue teaching in my spare time.

Whatever fear or doubt I harbored before I started my journey had turned into love and faith, and gave me the courage to do things I never imagined myself doing.

Like surprising my mother on her 70th birthday in London.

I planned her surprise with the help of my father, who had bought plane tickets to London for her and my sister. But the highlight was surprising my Mom at Heathrow Airport.

Even though I left San Francisco the night before, I wasn't sure everything would fall into place like it did. After a 10-hour flight, I landed in Heathrow exactly one hour before my mother and sister, so I managed to prepare a "Happy Birthday" sign and was there to greet them in the passenger hall.

You can imagine my mom's shock when she came out of the terminal and saw me waiting for them. She froze, and while a crowd of passengers passed her by, she stood there until it finally sunk in that it really was me there waiting for her. We finally fell into each other's arms, my mom pinching me to make sure she wasn't dreaming.

I had visited London the first time in 1995, to celebrate my honeymoon, and here I was in London again for my mom's 70th birthday. Only this time I was happier and more complete than ever. I don't know if I would call it a corrective experience, but rather a personal and unique experience of who I really am – authentic, spontaneous; real.

And it was perfect.

From the moment I landed in London in time to greet them and surprise my mom in the passenger hall, everything was perfect.

I rented an apartment for us in the most popular and hippest area in London – Covent Garden, and on the first night we celebrated at an upscale restaurant of a famous Israeli chef. Delicious food, amazing service, and a warm atmosphere, all topped with a "Happy Birthday" song and a cake with candle. Awesome B-day party!

On our first day, the weather was beautiful and sunny, and we enjoyed walking on the streets of London. We had a lovely stroll towards Buckingham Palace, a 20-minute walk from our apartment, followed by many other sites that we managed to tour that same day.

That night I wrote in my journal:

> "Happiness! It is just pure joy to see my mother so happy, to see my sister so happy, and to enjoy these magical moments with them here in London.
>
> We started our day at the palace, watching the changing of the guards, and then took a taxi boat to the Tower of London. We visited the London Bridge and The Shard (the 95-story skyscraper formerly known as London Bridge Tower), where we had a toast in front of a 360° panoramic view. We

ended with a late dinner at an Indian restaurant in Covent Garden and then watched *Notting Hill*, which just happened to be on TV tonight!

The three of us are living a dream! And through others I continue to learn how to be in the moment, to bring everyone to the moment and to be joyous!

Good night in London."

October 5th, 2018

The next morning, we took the London Underground for the first time, and, since my mother's boots tore when she "minded the gap," we headed straight to Harrods to buy her a new pair. It was a perfect choice for a rainy day, and we enjoyed every moment of our shopping experience.

That night we went to see the *Phantom of the Opera*. We walked into the beautiful Her Majesty's Theatre, all dressed up, each holding a glass of champagne, and took our seats in the front rows. When the lights came down and the music started playing, I could almost hear the excited beating of our hearts. We laughed, cried, and loved every moment of it until the perfect ending.

We spent our last night jogging around the neighborhood, discovering new places and enjoying the beauty of the city at night. We hardly slept that night. Wanting to take advantage of every last hour together, we stayed up talking, sitting on the bed, opening up to each other, listening to each other, and bonding even more.

Even though I scarcely slept that night, I got up early the next morning and went to a yoga class at a local studio so that I could experience yoga in that part of the world as well. I didn't want to miss the thing that had become an inseparable part of me, part of the woman who returned to London after 23 years, the one thing I carry with me wherever I go in the world – yoga.

I came back to our apartment, sweaty and happy to have practiced yoga in London, and we all packed our bags and headed for the airport. Grateful for our time together, I said goodbye to my mother and my sister and boarded my flight back to San Francisco, as they waited for their flight back to Tel Aviv.

This was a magical trip, an inspiring reunion and a once-in-a-lifetime experience!

Chapter 27: 108 Sun Salutations

I LANDED IN SAN FRANCISCO, happy to come back to the boys who were waiting for me at home with our loving dog Sky. Of course, I didn't come back empty-handed. I brought them presents from grandma; t-shirts and vinyl records of their favorite bands – The Beatles and Pink Floyd.

As a mother of two teenage boys, I felt pretty lucky that they were so responsible and mature for their age, and that despite the fact that they were already 15, my relationship with them only grew stronger and we had many common interests – music, movies and swimming.

We had a Thanksgiving tradition of getting into the car with Sky and driving without a specific destination. Whenever we reached an intersection, one of us would choose which way to turn. We all took turns and drove until it got dark. Once it got dark, we would look for a place to spend the night, and the next morning we would head back home.

This custom may sound crazy and irresponsible, but every year we ended up discovering an exciting new place.

When we returned from our most recent adventure, I wrote in my journal:

> "Tonight, we returned from our family journey into the unknown, something

we've been doing for years. We go nowhere and then we get somewhere.

Yesterday was rainy, and it was a little scary to be on the roads, but we played a cool song game and didn't want to stop anywhere.

When it got dark, we ended up finding this really lavish and lovely hotel at a crossroads near the Sacramento River. Lucky for us, they are pet-friendly and had one room left. It was dreamy, hanging out in the Jacuzzi while it was raining outside, having dinner at the hotel restaurant, and watching a movie in our room.

In the morning, I practiced yoga and we went hiking, walked the steel, glass and granite Sundial Bridge, visited the Turtle Bay Exploration Park and Museum, and then headed home, enjoying a lot of laughs on the way.

I am thankful for this magical quality time with my two sons and my beloved dog. Thankful for the closeness, the love, the warmth, and this special bond between us that grows stronger, even today, when they are 15 years old.

What a road trip!"

November 24th, 2018

The following month, during their winter break from school, we established another family tradition – we went to Israel to celebrate my father's 78th birthday, and to welcome the New Year at the Western Wall in the Holy City of Jerusalem.

The highlight of our trip for me was practicing the 108 Sun Salutations with my sister on the last day of the year – December 31st, 2018 – at a yoga studio in Tel Aviv.

The yoga lesson "108 Sun Salutations" is given once a year only, on the verge of the New Year. During the lesson we repeat the same action 108 times; 108 sequences of Vinyasa, also known as the Sun Salutation.

Aside from the physical endeavor, which left our muscles tight and sore for days, I also felt that with every sequence I was shedding another layer of unwanted weight. In a way, I was leaving behind everything that wasn't serving me anymore, beginning the New Year with a clean slate, feeling so much lighter.

The number 108 is not arbitrary. In astrology, the number 108 is quite significant. In fact, in India they used to describe distances and sizes by using the sun and the moon as reference points. They found that the average distance between Earth and the sun is 108 times the diameter of the sun, and the average distance between Earth and the moon is 108 times the diameter of the moon.

They also found that the diameter of the sun is 108 times the diameter of Earth.

The sun and the moon are meaningful symbols in Indian tradition. The sun represents the mental energy, the consciousness, and the moon represents the Prana – the life force, the breath. Hatha yoga, which focuses on practicing with the physical body as a way to release the consciousness and unite with the divine, is actually two words – "Ha" is the sun and "Tha" is the moon. These two represent the two basic and opposing energies within us. It is believed that when there is balance and union between these two energies, the divine spark awakens within us.

Yoga further teaches that when we practice the Sun Salutation 108 times, or say a certain mantra 108 times, we get a little bit closer to the light and the divine energy.

The greatest gift of all was given to me at the end of the practice, when our yoga teacher read to us a prayer called the "Prayer of the Soul."

It moved me to tears, and since then, I've said it every morning at the end of my yoga practice.

"Dear Lord,

Here I am forgiving myself
for all the moments I abandoned myself
and gave others the power to hurt me and break
    me to pieces.

For seeking love and recognition from strangers
For looking at myself in the eyes of others.

Here I am forgiving myself
for all the time I have wasted on thoughts of other
    people's thoughts.
For believing the lies and thinking for one moment
that I wasn't loved or worthy of this beautiful life.

Here I am forgiving myself
for making a place in my heart for words
that hurt more than knives, and
for making a place in my heart for the weakness of
    others.

I embrace myself, and
hug myself and respect who I am
and the child in me.

I am hereby regaining my strength
and making a place free of judgment.
A place where I can return to from all distances
At any given moment, at any second, at any hour
    of the day
A place where I am always loved and dear.

I am building a home for myself in my heart
and accept all the parts of me
and love and love unconditionally.

I am hereby regaining my strength
and releasing weights and heavy loads
anger, resentment and hatred that block me

from this blessing and the joy that I deserve.

I hereby set myself free and forgive myself
and anyone who has sinned or acted against me."

Chapter 28: Dreams Do Come True

IN 2018, MY JOURNEY into the unknown continued an upward trend, with many surprises in store.

It was a year of birthday celebrations – my mom's in London and my dad's in Israel. A year of forgiveness and absolution – mainly forgiving myself. A year of freedom and release from the things that no longer served me. A year rich with new experiences that made me look forward to whatever came next.

I welcomed the New Year with a fascinating and meaningful encounter with an Indian doctor who specializes in Ayurveda medicine.

Ayurveda, meaning "knowledge of life" in Sanskrit, is the world's most ancient medicine and surgery. It originated in India more than 5,000 years ago, and is often called the "Mother of All Healing."

As is evident from its name, Ayurveda is a way of life for healing the body through nutrition, medicinal herbs, stress reduction, balancing the digestive system, and maintaining a healthy lifestyle.

The ayurvedic healer I was longing to meet comes to the US once a year, and so I had to schedule my appointment with him months in advance. On the Saturday of my appointment, February 10th, 2019, I woke up early, vibrating with excitement, and drove 75 miles north to a town called Fairfax, an hour drive from San Francisco.

My appointment was at 9 a.m., and at that point I had fasted for 12 hours in order to get a precise diagnosis of my pulse and my tongue.

As strange as it may sound, it turns out that it's possible to know exactly what's going on in the body just by looking at the tongue. And by listening to our pulse, the healer can detect if we are off-balance.

I got there at 8:50 a.m. and sat in the waiting room, awaiting my turn with anxiety and anticipation. The door opened and a tall, tan man in his forties greeted me. I was confused for a moment as to whether this was the Indian healer or his assistant.

I looked at him again. "He doesn't look Indian," I thought.

He looked completely American, or to be precise – he looked like a surfer from San Diego who spends most of his time at the beach.

As I continued to admire this attractive man standing in front of me, he extended his hand to shake mine, and introduced himself.

"Nice to meet you, I'm Dr. Nibodhi."

Dr. Nibodhi invited me into the examination room and sat down on a meditation pillow on the floor. I moved the pillow that was next to him and sat down on the floor in front of him.

Trying my best to conceal how shocked I was, I looked around me to avoid eye contact. Could it be that this was the illustrious healer everyone was recommending and talking about? How could it be? He's so young!

With a soft, pleasant voice, he asked me to give him my hand, and then the room went silent while he felt for the artery in my wrist in order to diagnose my pulse. I tried to be as still as I could and sit peacefully while he focused on my pulse. He then asked me to stick my tongue out and proceeded to look straight into my mouth.

When he was done, I took a deep breath and waited without much patience to hear his findings. Dr. Nibodhi took a blank form and started scribbling notes.

"My wife will be in shortly with a cup of ginger tea so you may break the fast," he said quietly and continued scribbling.

"You're very dehydrated. You don't drink enough water," he chided gently. "You eat very fast, you don't chew your food enough before you swallow it."

Then he asked, "You weren't breastfed, right?"

Amazed at the question, I answered, "That's right. I was born with a cleft lip, and from the day I was born my Mother fed me with a spoon."

177

"God gave us teeth to smile and to chew," he said, and asked that from now on I take the time to chew my food before I swallow it.

He explained that I was somewhat off balance and that I must abstain from wheat, potatoes, tomatoes and eggplant. He went on to explain that the reason I was getting sick pretty often and had a lot of sinus infections was because I was eating fruit with my meal. He asked that I make sure to eat fruit at least 90 minutes before my meal or two hours after it.

"You don't have onion in your body," he added.

I was shocked.

"I hate onions!" I exclaimed. "I don't even let them into my house!"

"But onion is your medicine, especially when cooked," he replied. "Cooked onion will strengthen your immune system and heal you.

"Do you ever fast?"

"No," I said. "Only once a year on Yom Kippur."

"You have to fast once a week in order to give your body a rest," he said. "God said that on the seventh day we stop everything and do nothing, but we don't even give our body a day of rest. We're constantly eating."

He was pleased to hear that I practice yoga every day, and recommended I also start meditating every night before bed.

"I want you to close the day with meditation before you fall asleep," he said. "Your sleep is troubled, and in order to leave the day behind and go to sleep with a clean mind, you must sit and meditate for at least 15 to 30 minutes and reflect on everything you went through that day. I promise, you will sleep like a baby. A deep, quality sleep.

"I want you to hug a tree every day, or at least once a week. Trees have so many qualities, and when we hug them, we get closer to nature, our immune system is strengthened, and we derive a lot of power from the trees."

"Are you serious?" I asked doubtfully.

He looked at me and said, "Very serious."

Before we parted, Dr. Nibodhi assured me that if I followed his instructions, I would feel stronger and more vital.

"You will see, your hair will strengthen, and your teeth will be much healthier. You will feel 30 years younger, and I'm sure that the next time we meet, you will be full of energy and will feel on top of the world."

He stood up and smiled with his hands pressed together in "namaste."

I smiled back and thanked him for the comprehensive education and advice.

After leaving the healer's room with a page filled with specific instructions about the changes I needed to make in my nutrition and my lifestyle, I looked for a place to get a bite to eat before the drive home. I stopped at a local cafe and had a salad, while trying to absorb everything Dr. Nibodhi said.

My head was full of new information. I stared at the long list of what to eat and what not to eat, when to eat, when to go to bed, when to wake up, when to fast (once a week!) and a thousand other things I needed to do.

I took a deep breath and stopped to think.

I know myself – it's all or nothing for me. Either I took what he said and fully implement it, or give up the idea completely and get on with my life as it was. And then I remembered his promise, and in that moment, I decided to take all of his recommendations and follow them through. I had nothing to lose and everything to gain. Yes, it would take a strong commitment on my part and some persistence, but if there was a chance I might feel better, physically and mentally, then I deemed it well worth the effort.

From that day on I changed my nutritional habits and my lifestyle according to Dr. Nibodhi's recommendations.

I hugged the tree in my front yard every morning, even though the neighbors thought I was nuts, and made it a habit to fast every Friday, never missing one.

In less than two weeks I could already feel the difference. I lost those extra 10 pounds I didn't need, I slept like a baby at night and had endless energy and youthful vigor. A sense of wholeness filled my heart. Just as he promised, I wasn't getting sick anymore. Even when the boys got the flu in the winter, I stayed strong and resistant.

Just as Dr. Nibodhi predicted, I felt on top of the world.

A month after my meeting with Dr. Nibodhi, my parents came for a surprise visit to celebrate my 46th birthday on March 12th, 2019. They landed in San Francisco airport on March 10th, looking younger than ever and excited for my birthday.

My father was the first to notice the change in me. "You have the body of a 16-year-old girl!" he exclaimed.

My mom, seeing my calm and peaceful expression, said, "My child, you have arrived."

I remembered the last time they visited, right before my divorce. I always regretted that visit leaving a bad taste in their mouths, more so after what my father had told me when he landed in San Francisco – "This is the last time I'm taking this horrible flight. I feel like I aged 10 years."

I always dreamed that maybe one day, my parents would visit again. And now, after a lot of water under the bridge, that day had come!

"Dreams do come true," I thought, on my birthday. What a huge present it was to have my parents here with me. This time would be a better experience for them, they would be able to see how happy I was in my home, and how I was surrounded with so much love.

When we came from the airport to my fully renovated house, it looked nothing like the house they remembered. Their eyes gleamed as they walked in and inhaled the calm and peaceful atmosphere.

We kicked off my birthday celebrations with a trip to Mendocino, followed by dinners and parties with friends and neighbors who all came to welcome and meet those famous parents I spoke so much about, the most wonderful parents in the world!

The two weeks they were here felt like a dream. Each morning I would pinch myself to make sure I wasn't dreaming.

Their visit inspired me to make one more dream come true, not my own, but my kids'. In complete secrecy, I started planning a special 16th birthday trip to London. After all, when I got back from my trip to London with my mom, I promised to take them there someday. I bet they didn't expect that "someday" would happen so quickly.

In July the three of us flew to London. It was my sons' first visit to Europe, and an opportunity for me to overcome my fear and travel abroad with them as a single mom.

After touring London, we took a train to Liverpool, the music capital of Europe, and birthplace of The Beatles.

It was wonderful, discovering new places with them.

Yes, dreams do come true.

Chapter 29: The Journey to Inner Peace and Delight

WHEN I TOLD MY FATHER I was writing a book about my journey, he asked that I remember to share some of the great stories from my childhood.

"You had a lovely childhood," he said. "You have to write about those years."

I'm sure my father remembers many things that I've forgotten, or chose to forget about my childhood, but there is one story that was particularly memorable.

When my mom was pregnant with my sister, I felt like the world had come to an end, and the birth of my sister meant that I would lose the spotlight and be left behind, abandoned to my fate.

One morning at recess, I tripped and hurt my knee. My friends tried to help me up, but I screamed in pain and asked them to take me to the school nurse. The nurse looked at my knee and asked if I could stand on that leg. Still in terrible pain, I told her I could neither stand nor walk. The nurse called my mother and asked her to come right away. My mom came as quickly as she could, and following the nurse's recommendation, took me to the nearest ER so that a doctor could see me.

My mom, who was heavily pregnant and didn't have a car, carried me all the way to the ER, worried that I might have broken my leg. We arrived at the hospital and waited for half an hour in the hallway for the doctor to arrive.

When he came in, he came straight to us to see what had happened. "Sweetheart, could you show me where it hurts?" he asked.

I looked down at my legs and pointed to my right leg. Then I hesitated, "Wait, I think it may be the other leg…"

The doctor looked at me, puzzled, and my mother said, "You've already forgotten which leg was hurting?!"

"Mom, I think it's this one," I said sheepishly, pointing at one of them.

My mom apologized to the doctor, grabbed my hand and led me outside.

"You let me carry you all the way here, and apparently you can walk perfectly on both legs!" she said furiously.

As we walked home, I tried to explain to my mother that it passed and it didn't hurt so much anymore, but my mother was exhausted and preferred not to argue. She walked all the way home in complete silence.

You must think I was a horrible child. What kind of child does that to her mom? And I would definitely agree, but I was only eight years old, needy, and very manipulative.

That girl grew up to be a needy woman who believed that without affirmation from the outside world, she didn't exist. My habit of using manipulation to get the attention and closeness I so desperately needed and craved continued well into my adulthood.

I never liked that side of me. I'm ashamed to admit that I spent most of my life looking at myself through the eyes of others. But after forgiving myself, I realized that one of the most important things I've learned in my journey is that the only absolute truth is happiness.

When we delude ourselves, we forget that we are already happy, and then we begin to look for it from outside ourselves. Happiness is always within us. The moment we forget the truth of our own true self, we are deluded. No one can make us happy and no one can make us unhappy. Nothing on earth can bring us what we already have, and nothing can take it away from us, unless we choose to let it go.

Not needing anyone is one of the most liberating things in the world, and knowing and believing that my happiness is in my hands alone brought that huge transformation. I turned from a needy woman into an independent woman who found happiness on her own.

So, yes, my boys are 17 now, and their friends say I'm not like other mothers.

"Mom, my friends asked me how come you're always smiling and happy. 'What is she on? Drugs? She's always so energetic, and she always looks high.' I told them it's yoga."

I truly believe that it is because I was persistent in the way I chose to deal with life. Life will always toss us around, the question is, how will we deal with surprises along the way?

With this same belief, I continue my nightly tradition of saying the same mantra 108 times. The only thing that changed is my mantra. It is no longer Hari Om. My new mantra is –

L O V E

This mantra is deeply meaningful to me and it fills me with a deep love for life, for the world and for everyone around me. This mantra reminds me that the most important thing is self-love. To be friends with all the parts of me, and to love even those sides I'm not too proud of.

So, where do we go from here? Nobody really knows.

All we can do is be open and curious about all the things that await us along the way. To never give up our happiness, and to realize that it is all in our hands.

For the first time in my life, I am excited for the future, and with an open heart I step forward, continuing my journey into the unknown...

Chapter 30: My First Poem

HAPPINESS.

Happiness is to speak your truth
Happiness is to be authentic
Happiness is to be myself
Happiness is to be happy for others
Happiness is to see the beauty in everything
Happiness is to forgive without holding a grudge
Happiness is to not seek validation
Happiness is to be HERE and not wanting to be anywhere
    else but HERE
Happiness is to be satisfied
Happiness is to feel whole
Happiness is to feel full even when I am hungry
Happiness is to feel free
Happiness is to be calm even in a storm
Happiness is to have faith and not to worry
Happiness is to accept and not resist
Happiness is to hug the pain lovingly
Happiness is to LOVE
Happiness is to GIVE
Happiness is to share the JOY
Happiness is to not be afraid
Happiness is to trust and believe that it always exists.

About the Author

Yonit Cohen was born and raised in Israel. She moved with her family to the Silicon Valley in 2000, and now lives in San Francisco with her twin teenaged sons. In her teens, Yonit studied acting, and holds a bachelor's degree in accounting and business management. She is a yoga and meditation instructor, an RYT® 200, and a member of Yoga Alliance®.

Yonit's life mission is to create trust through cultivating vulnerability. Within her first book, she shares valuable insight and unfolds a rich life experience.

Connect with Yonit:
- Instagram: @yonityoga
- Website: www.yonitcohen.com

Made in the USA
Las Vegas, NV
14 August 2021

28188270R00114